# PARLIAMENTS

# EXPLORING WORLD GOVERNMENTS

**ABDO**
Publishing Company

# PARLIAMENTS

by Mary K. Pratt

**Content Consultant**
Delmer Lonowski,
Professor of Political Science
South Dakota
State University

# CREDITS

Printed in the United States of America,
North Mankato, Minnesota
112010
012011

♻ THIS BOOK CONTAINS AT LEAST 10% RECYCLED MATERIALS.

Editor: Melissa York
Copy Editor: Sarah Beckman
Interior Design and Production: Kazuko Collins
Cover Design: Becky Daum

Photo Credits: George Osborne/AP Images, cover, 2, 3; Chris Clark/AP Images, 9; Rui Vieira/AP Images, 14; Fotolia, 19; Asianet-Pakistan/Shutterstock Images, 26; Jens Dige/AP Images, 29; North Wind Picture Archives/AP Images, 33; Currier & Ives/Library of Congress, 37; Library of Congress, 43, 124; Gianluigi Guercia/AP Images, 53; Christopher Elwell/Shutterstock Images, 57; Alkis Konstantinidis/AP Images, 63; Isa Ismail/Shutterstock Images, 65; Shutterstock Images, 69, 116; Olga Besnard/Shutterstock Images, 77; Itsuo Inouye/AP Images, 79; Gustavo Ferrari/AP Images, 85; Karen Lau/Fotolia, 91; Johann Helgason/Shutterstock Images, 96; Renáta Sedmáková/Fotolia, 101; Aija Lehtonen/Shutterstock Images, 105; Alexander Kalina/Shutterstock Images, 113; Kyodo/AP Images, 121; Christopher Elwell/Shutterstock Images, 130; Musadeq Sadeq/AP Images, 133; Cedric Joubert/AP Images, 143

Library of Congress Cataloging-in-Publication Data
Pratt, Mary K.
  Parliaments / by Mary K. Pratt.
    p. cm. -- (Exploring world governments)
  Includes bibliographical references.
  ISBN 978-1-61714-793-7
  1. Legislative bodies--Juvenile literature. 2. Representative government and representation--Juvenile literature. I. Title.
  JF511.P73 2011
  328.3--dc22
                                                    2010045759

# Table of Contents

# What Is Government?

In the earliest, simplest societies, government as we know it did not exist. Family or tribal elders made decisions, and their powers were limited. As civilizations grew, governments developed to organize societies and to protect them from outside threats. As societies have grown in complexity, so have the governments that organize them. In this way, organizing society has led to massive bureaucracies with many offices and roles.

As of 2010, there were more than 190 countries, each with its own government. Two governments may look very similar on paper even though political life inside those countries varies greatly. Every government is different because it is influenced by its country's history, culture, economics, geography, and even psychology.

Still, governments share some main roles. Today, a main function of governments is to protect citizens from outside threats. This has evolved into the vast arena of international relations, including military alliances and trade agreements. Governments also organize power in a society. However, how power is acquired—through elections, heredity, or force—varies, as does who exercises it—one person, a few, or many.

Ideally, governments balance the rights of individuals against the needs of the whole society. But who defines those needs? Is it leaders chosen by universal suffrage, or is it a single dictator who assumed power through force? How are individual rights protected? The answers to these questions distinguish one form of government from another.

Another role of government is preserving internal order—that is, order as defined by those in power. While keeping order might mean prosecuting violent criminals in a democracy, in a dictatorship, it could mean prosecuting dissenters. Governments also look out for the welfare of their citizens. All modern governments provide some form of social services, ranging from education to housing to health care.

Governments are often involved in their national economies. Involvement can run the full spectrum—from completely planning the economy to merely levying taxes and allowing a free market to operate. Governments also regulate the private lives of citizens—from issuing marriage licenses in a democracy to enforcing specific styles of dress in a theocracy.

While all governments have some characteristics in common, the world's governments take many forms and make decisions differently. How does a government decide what individual rights to give its citizens? How are laws enforced? What happens when laws are broken? The answers to such questions depend on the political system at hand. ⌘

# 1

# A Parliament Renews Itself

**B**ritish citizens headed to the election polls in May 2010 to decide the future of their country. They were casting their votes for the candidates they wanted to serve in the 650-member House of Commons, one of two chambers that make up the British Parliament. Their decisions would determine the political makeup of that legislative body. They would vote for which party would lead the country, and that party would choose the prime minister.

The United Kingdom, similar to parliamentary governments around the world, holds

*Volunteers counted votes in Britain's 2010 general election.*

K
115

general elections every several years. When elections take place, Parliament is dissolved. That means every seat in the House of Commons becomes vacant, and voters must elect new members of Parliament, called MPs in the United Kingdom. The members of the second chamber, the House of Lords, are not elected. Instead, they are appointed by the British monarch. In the United Kingdom, each constituency, or voting district, elects one MP to a seat in the House of Commons. Although candidates who are not part of any political party can run as independents, the majority of candidates belong to a political party registered with the Electoral Commission. Normally, the political party that wins the majority of seats in the House of Commons gets to lead the government.

However, when the polls closed on May 7, 2010, and the voting was done, no political party had won a majority of seats. The Conservative Party, led by David Cameron, had captured 306 seats in the House of Commons. The Labour Party, which had governed the country for the previous 13 years, took 258 seats. The Liberal Democrats received only 57 seats. Smaller regional parties took the remaining 28 seats. A political party needs to capture 326 seats in the House of Commons to gain control. If no party gains this majority, the monarch invites the party with the most votes—in this case the Conservative Party— to form a coalition government. In other words, the Conservative Party would have to join forces with another party to have more than 326 seats and gain a majority in the House of Commons.

# A New Government Begins

After several days of negotiations, the Conservative Party joined with the Liberal Democrats to form a coalition government. It was the first time the two political parties had shared power in Parliament. It was also the first coalition government in the United Kingdom since World War II (1939–1945).

Similar to other coalition governments, the Conservative Party and the Liberal Democrats had to agree on how they would vote on important domestic issues, or issues that affect life in their own country. They also had to agree on foreign-policy points, which affect how they deal with other countries. They had to agree on certain key business and economic policy positions too. The result of this negotiation was a published policy agreement.

## DAVID CAMERON

When David Cameron took office in May 2010, he was only 43 years old. He was the youngest British prime minister in almost 200 years. Lord Liverpool held the post at age 42 in 1812.

Cameron's mother's family had produced a number of Conservative Party MPs through several generations. His godfather was also an MP. Cameron himself started with the Tories, as the Conservative Party is known, when he was young. Cameron was elected as a Conservative Party MP in 2001 and became a vice chairman of the Conservative Party in November 2003. He was elected leader of the Conservative Party on December 6, 2005, and he became prime minister nearly five years later.

However, the agreement showed that although the two parties shared power, they did not necessarily share ideology. For example, the two did not agree on all tax policies, but the parties had to find common ground to work together. The Conservatives agreed to support the Liberal Democrats' plan: Parliament would increase the minimum amount someone had to earn before paying income taxes. In addition, the parties agreed the Liberal Democrats could vote against some Conservative-sponsored tax breaks.

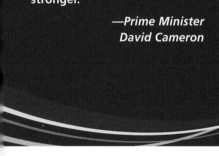

"I joined this party because I believe in freedom. We are the only party believing that if you give people freedom and responsibility, they will grow stronger and society will grow stronger."[1]

—*Prime Minister David Cameron*

Once the coalition formed, the former prime minister, Labour Party leader Gordon Brown, resigned from office, smoothing the way for the new government to take over. Power transferred peacefully from the Labour Party to the new coalition government, and one of the oldest operating political systems in the world remained intact.

As leader of the Conservative Party, Cameron became prime minister. The Liberal Democrats' leader, Nick Clegg, became deputy prime minister. Leaders from both parties were appointed to the other 21 cabinet positions. Conservative members took 17 posts, including chancellor, home secretary, and foreign secretary. Liberal Democrats were appointed to the remaining four cabinet posts.

In a press conference announcing the coalition, Cameron said the two parties shared several beliefs that were important for sharing power. He said they both supported "three key principles—freedom, fairness, and responsibility."[2]

Cameron also said at the press conference that the two parties would work together "to give our country the strong and stable and determined leadership that we need for the long

## WHAT IS A CABINET?

A cabinet is made up of ministers, or appointed government leaders. In many countries, they are appointed by the prime minister. The ministers are in charge of key policy areas, such as defense, education, and foreign policy. In the United Kingdom, as in other parliamentary governments, the ministers are top leaders in the ruling political party. Most often, the prime minister selects cabinet members who are also members of parliament. In the United Kingdom, for example, the prime minister selects cabinet members from his or her party or coalition. However, prime ministers in some countries select cabinet members who are not members of the elected chamber of parliament.

The cabinet meets regularly with the prime minister to offer advice and implement public policies. How much power the cabinet has varies by country. Some cabinets aid in making executive decisions, while others have far less influence over the governing prime ministers.

*British Prime Minister David Cameron,
right, and Deputy Prime Minister Nick
Clegg spoke together on October 21, 2010.*

term" and that they would "take Britain in a
historic new direction, a direction of hope and
unity, conviction and common purpose."[3]

# Early Challenges to the Coalition

The new British government set to work immediately. Parliament faced early challenges, particularly regarding taxes and government spending, which tested the coalition partners. It had to establish its positions in relation to other world leaders and foreign governments.

At the time, the country's debt was growing very quickly. The coalition partners agreed that tackling the growing fiscal deficit was a priority. Cameron blamed the former ruling Labour Party for reckless spending, which contributed to the problem. He said he wanted to cut government spending on public programs to save money and to help trim the deficit. He said his fiscal policies would affect every citizen in the United Kingdom. "Around the world people and their governments are waking up to the dangers of not dealing with their debts. And Britain must be part of that international mainstream," Cameron said.[4]

But Deputy Prime Minister Nick Clegg changed the tone of the rhetoric when he said the government would not return to the harsh spending restraints of former prime minister Margaret Thatcher, a Conservative who governed from 1979 to 1990. "Fiscal retrenchment does not mean a repeat of the 1980s. We are going to do this differently," Clegg said.[5]

Coalition governments, which are more common in other countries governed by parliaments, only work when the political parties get along. For instance, while the Conservatives and the Liberal Democrats were coming together in the United Kingdom, the coalition government in Germany's parliament was in danger of coming apart. The ruling parties—the Christian Democratic Union, the Christian Social Union, and the Free Democratic Party—fell into disagreement over taxes and government spending. When coalitions fall apart, the government must call for new elections.

The parliamentary governments of the world share many characteristics, such as an elected legislative body and a prime minister who acts as head of government. In many ways, the United Kingdom's 2010 election is representative of how a parliamentary government works. Cooperation is essential to parliamentary governments.

## AT A GLANCE: THE UNITED KINGDOM

- An electoral democracy.
- Governed by a parliament, called UK Parliament or Parliament.
- The House of Commons is the lower house and the dominant one. Its members are elected.
- The House of Lords is the upper house. Its members are appointed by the monarch.
- Queen Elizabeth II is the reigning monarch. The monarch serves as head of state, a largely ceremonial role.
- The two largest political parties are the Conservative Party and the Labour Party. Smaller parties include the Liberal Democrats, the Welsh Nationalist Party (also called Plaid Cymru), and the Scottish National Party.

A parliament must respond to the people, or it will be dissolved. Even though many countries share a parliamentary system of government, each nation's government has its own traditions, customs, practices, and laws. ⌘

# 2

# What Is a Parliamentary Government?

**A** parliamentary government is one in which the lawmaking group, called the parliament, has the power to make and execute laws. The country's leader, usually called the prime minister, is a member of the parliament. This is unlike the United States, which has a presidential system in which Congress (the legislative branch) makes the laws, while the president (the executive branch) executes or carries them out.

*Westminster Palace in London is home to Britain's Parliament.*

There are several different types of parliamentary governments, but the most recognizable form is the system used in the United Kingdom. The British system of parliamentary government is also known as the Westminster parliamentary model. It is so called because the building that houses the British Parliament is called Westminster Palace. In this model, the prime minister is the leader of the political party that holds the majority of seats in the elected House of Commons.

## How Parliaments Are Elected

The Westminster model and other parliamentary systems in democratic countries are based on the principle of regularly held elections. In these

## CHARACTERISTICS OF PARLIAMENTARY SYSTEMS

Democratic parliamentary systems have several key characteristics that set them apart from other forms of government:

- The legislature and executive are fused.
- The leader of the majority party or coalition in parliament becomes the prime minister.
- In most countries, the prime minister chooses the members of the cabinet.
- The prime minister usually chooses cabinet members from the majority party or, in the case of a coalition government, the parties that make up the coalition.
- The prime minister remains in power until he or she calls for a general election or is forced to dissolve parliament after a vote of no confidence.

elections, eligible citizens vote for the individuals they want to hold office. Many parliaments do not have fixed timeframes for elections, which is something that separates this form of government from the presidential model used in the United States. Instead, countries with parliaments generally require elections to be held every four or five years.

In the United Kingdom, voters in each geographic region, called a constituency, elect one MP. If one political party wins a majority of seats, then it forms the next ruling government. If one political party does not win a majority of seats, then the party with the most seats must negotiate with at least one other party to form a coalition. The leader of the ruling party or coalition becomes the prime minister.

Voters in countries with typical parliamentary governments do not directly elect a prime minister. However, voters know that the prime minister is the leader of the political party that wins the most seats. So as they cast their votes for the party they want, they are also casting a vote for the leader who will be selected as prime minister.

## What Parliaments Do

Members of most parliaments have several main jobs: to debate the issues affecting the country, to make laws, and to determine how public money is spent. Members of parliament often present their own as well as their constituents' feelings about suggested laws and policies put before the parliament. They argue about the perceived merits and drawbacks to measures. They question the prime minister about his or her actions and policies. The debate often follows the style of debate seen in the US Congress, with members of parliament speaking along their party lines on whether they support or oppose a measure and giving the reasons why. After the debate, members of parliament cast their votes. The bill then passes or fails based on whether enough parliament members approve it. Members of parliament also serve as public stewards, watching over the prime minister and government offices to ensure they are operating effectively.

There are many similarities between parliaments around the world and the US Congress. Similar to members of parliaments, members of Congress are generally members of political parties, although occasionally some are elected as independents. Similar to the political alliances

## POLITICAL PARTIES

A political party can be defined as a group organized to win and exercise power. Party members generally share a political ideology. They work together to define their positions on important issues facing them individually and collectively as a society. They work together to support candidates for election to parliament as well as local government boards. They also work to persuade other citizens to support their candidates and their positions on the issues.

that exist in parliaments, members of Congress often vote along party lines.

However, there is one significant difference between the US government and Westminster-style parliamentary governments. In the United States, the president is separately elected. The president cannot be a member of Congress, and the president's political party does not have to be the party that holds the majority of seats in Congress. This creates a system of checks and balances between the legislative body and the executive branch in the US government that does not exist in parliamentary government.

## The Prime Minister and Cabinet

Under the parliamentary model, the prime minister is considered the head of the government. The prime minister generally chooses cabinet members from members of the ruling party or parties and decides which positions each one will occupy. The prime minister and the cabinet serve as the ruling party's leaders, and they make up the government's executive branch.

Cabinet members oversee various government departments or ministries. A cabinet member acts as the executive of that department, and civil servants carry out the policies, spending, and administration of each department. The prime minister sets the agenda for cabinet decisions and actions and generally determines the government's overall direction.

In addition to overseeing their specific areas, cabinet members help the prime minister make and execute new laws. The prime minister and cabinet members set legislative priorities by deciding how to handle important issues or how to allocate resources. Members of parliament in some countries using the Westminster model or a variation of it are not allowed to propose legislation that requires spending public money; only cabinet members may do that. This type of restriction reinforces the executive branch's position of power.

## CIVIL SERVANTS

Cabinet members oversee departments or ministries, but civil servants carry out the day-to-day tasks. Civil servants are often career professionals working in government, and they possess a great deal of knowledge about the areas of government in which they work. They sometimes use that knowledge to help cabinet members shape their public policies. The influence of civil servants in policy making varies by country. In France, for instance, senior civil servants have a significant level of participation in decision making and may serve as cabinet members.

## Members of Parliament and the Executive

Members of parliament can also have significant power relative to the executive branch. Members of parliament elect the prime minister, and they are unlikely to select a prime minister who disagrees with the agenda established by the party or coalition of parties that elected him or her to the office.

The parliament can also oust the prime minister and cabinet

through confidence motions. The government (that is, the ruling party or the ruling coalition parties) can demand a vote of confidence in support of the prime minister, while opposition political parties (those parties that do not hold a majority of the seats) can call for a vote of no confidence. If these motions show that most legislators do not have confidence in the ruling government, the government must resign. The prime minister steps down, and parliament is dissolved. A caretaker cabinet, which in some countries means the existing cabinet, takes charge until a new government is elected or formed.

## A VOTE OF NO CONFIDENCE

Some countries with a parliamentary government require very little to present no-confidence motions to the legislature. In Norway, for example, a single legislator can propose a no-confidence vote. Other countries require many more legislators to support putting the motion to a vote before action can be taken.

In many countries, the prime minister and the cabinet initiate proposals for new laws and policies, while parliament is responsible for approving them. Prime ministers work hard to persuade members in parliament to support their initiatives.

If the prime minister's party has a large majority, it is easier to pass legislation than if the majority is small or if a coalition government is in power. In the United Kingdom, for example,

The prime minister of Pakistan, Syed Yousuf Raza Gilani, right, met with an adviser in 2010.

either the Conservative Party or the Labour Party generally wins a majority of seats and rarely needs to join with another party to form a government. The prime minister generally can rely on a high level of support from his or her party, which gives the prime minister a high level of influence. In contrast, in coalition governments, the prime minister must work with the various parties to reach consensus and maintain support. That puts much more power into the legislators' hands.

## Constitutions

A constitution is a written document that establishes the procedures and rules by which its government operates. It explains the duties and powers of government offices and governing bodies. The US Constitution lays out how the US government works, but the United States is not the only country whose government is outlined by a constitution. Most countries with parliamentary governments also have constitutions contained in a single written document. The United Kingdom, Israel, and New Zealand are some notable exceptions.

A country's constitution generally contains more than the rules for how the government works. A constitution may also contain other rules that govern society. It often establishes the civil rights enjoyed by its citizens.

Various types of laws can also dictate a government's operations. Parliaments can pass statutes that create new policies and regulations, such as rules regarding environmental protection or rules on how corporations can conduct business. In the British example, custom and tradition play a major role.

Case law established by courts and judges can also set laws that affect how a government is run. The role of the judiciary in parliamentary governments varies. In most democratic parliamentary countries, such as Australia and Germany, the judiciary has the ability to declare laws unconstitutional, similar to the United States. In some exceptions, such as the United Kingdom, the judiciary cannot overturn laws passed by parliament.

However, some governments adhere to neither the country's constitution nor its statutory or case laws. Parliaments that support dictators or other types of authoritarian rule, for example, often operate outside the boundaries set by the laws of the land.

# Head of Government or Head of State

In the United States, the president is the sole national leader. The president leads the government, serves as the head of state, and acts as the country's face to the world. In parliamentary systems, these functions are often divided among two or more people. Although the prime minister is in charge of government, the prime minister in parliamentary systems is not considered the

## THE BRITISH MONARCHY

The role of Queen Elizabeth II in the United Kingdom also exemplifies how a monarch acts in a modern parliamentary system. As British sovereign, Queen Elizabeth is both head of state and head of the nation.

As head of state, Queen Elizabeth fulfills duties that developed during the past 1,000 years. Her domestic duties include opening Parliament, signing acts of Parliament, and meeting with the prime minister. She also has foreign duties, which include receiving foreign ambassadors and high commissioners, entertaining visiting heads of state, and visiting other nations as the representative of the United Kingdom.

As head of the nation, Queen Elizabeth plays an important part in her country's social and cultural realm. The queen serves as a focus for national unity—an individual and institution that citizens can rally around. As the monarch, she also creates a symbol of stability and continuity. Governments and prime ministers may change, but the monarchy remains. Queen Elizabeth also visits residents throughout the country and participates in celebrations and national ceremonies. For example, she takes part in the annual commemoration of deceased military veterans on Remembrance Sunday, which is a holiday similar to Veterans Day in the United States.

*Queen Margrethe II is the head of state for Denmark's parliamentary government.*

head of state. That title generally falls to another individual. For instance, Japan is a constitutional monarchy with a parliamentary government, and Emperor Akihito is its head of state. In other countries with parliamentary governments, the role of head of state is often held by an elected president.

The duties of the head of state vary from country to country and depend on several factors. Tradition and a country's constitution shape the role. Many duties are ceremonial. The head of state in countries with parliamentary systems often acts as a symbol of the nation and carries out diplomatic duties. Many heads of state also have the responsibility of ceremonially discharging parliament or asking the political party leaders to form the government. In Denmark, for example, Queen Margrethe II invites the party leader who has the support of the largest number of seats in the Danish parliament to form the government. She formally appoints the prime minister once the government is formed. She also signs all acts of parliament, but a cabinet member needs to countersign them before those acts can become law.

In Greece, the president is elected by the parliament. The Greek president once wielded greater power, but since the constitution was revised in 1986, the role has become mostly ceremonial.

Although there are differences in how parliaments work in each country, they share some fundamental structures. For example, in most parliaments, a party must hold a majority of seats or form a coalition to take power, and most parliaments have a prime minister who acts as head of government. How each country's parliament operates, how its members are elected, who serves as head of state, and how duties are divided are often a function of each country's history and culture. Despite these differences, parliamentary government still remains an enduring form of government that works in various regions and differing cultures. Its success stands as a testament to its adjustability, stability, and workability. ⌘

# 3

# Parliaments in History

**N**o one individual or group is responsible for founding and developing the parliamentary form of government. This is true even in the United Kingdom, where the system has a long and rich history. Rather, the government evolved through history as events and needs unfolded.

The modern British Parliament can trace its roots back to the eighth century. Starting at that time, the king called his leading advisers and nobles together to consult with them about matters affecting the country. This kind of meeting was called a Witan. Even though its

*King John of England signed the Magna Carta in 1215.*

main function was to offer advice to the king, he did not have to follow the group's guidance. However, most kings realized they needed the support of these advisers and nobles, as well as their loyal followers. So the kings had to balance their ability to defy the Witan's advice with their desire to maintain the group's continued support.

After the Norman Conquest in 1066, the king relied more heavily on a permanent council of advisers. This inner circle of confidants was called the Great Council. The Great Council is the historical basis of the upper house of the British Parliament, which is also known as the modern House of Lords.

The nobles, however, were often in disagreement with the kings and how they ruled. The nobles seized more power in 1215 when they forced King John to sign the Magna Carta, or great charter. The Magna Carta was a list of legal rights that forced King John and all subsequent monarchs to listen to the advice of the barons. Most important, the Magna Carta

## THE MONARCHY AND PARLIAMENT

King Henry VIII explained the relationship between the monarchy and Parliament in 1543 in an address to the House of Commons. He used the pronoun *we* to refer to himself.

*We as head, and you as members, are conjoined and knit together into one body politic, so as whatsoever offence or injury is offered to the meanest member of the House is to be judged as done against our person and the whole Court of Parliament.*[1]

reinforced the idea that the king needed to have the consent of the barons to collect taxes.

The word *parliament* was first used to describe these meetings of the king and the barons in 1236 by King Henry III, who reigned from 1216 to 1272. In addition to asking the barons for money, he also had to ask the counties, villages, and clergy directly. The idea evolved that the barons spoke for themselves, but the local leaders spoke for the people. This was the root of the House of Commons.

Parliament evolved in the following decades and centuries as subsequent kings continued to regularly order elections of the people's representatives, call Parliament into session, and ask

## THE MAGNA CARTA

One of the most important documents in the history of democracy is the Magna Carta. This thirteenth-century document established the rights of the people of England and bound the country's monarchy to honor them. Bowing to the demands of the noble barons, King John of England in 1215 agreed to the terms and rights laid out in the Magna Carta. He made the document the supreme law of the land and bound all his heirs to honor the rights the Magna Carta described. Written in Latin, the document served as the foundation of many of the rights that free societies, including the United States, enjoy in the twenty-first century. As former British prime minister Winston Churchill said in 1956:

*Here is a law which is above the King and which even he must not break. This reaffirmation of a supreme law and its expression in a general charter is the great work of Magna Carta; and this alone justifies the respect in which men have held it.*[2]

for taxes. By the early fourteenth century, the city representatives were a regular part of Parliament, and they were known as the House of Commons by 1332. The fourteenth century also saw the precursor of the prime minister. In 1376, the House of Commons elected a spokesman to represent members in front of the king.

## English Civil War

The road to the modern parliament was not always smooth. King Charles I, who came to power in 1625, believed he did not need the advice and consent of Parliament. Parliament did not share this belief. The balance of power

### OLIVER CROMWELL

One of the towering figures in British parliamentary history is Oliver Cromwell. Born in 1599 in Huntingdon, England, Cromwell attended a local school. After getting married, he farmed his family's small estate. It was there that he became active in local affairs and developed a reputation as a champion of the poor. He became active in Parliament in 1640, during the reign of Charles I. At this time, Parliament was critical of the king and sought to limit the king's and the Anglican Church's power. Cromwell supported these goals.

The struggle between Parliament and the king resulted in a civil war, during which Cromwell demonstrated military and leadership skills. On June 26, 1650, following the execution of Charles I and more than a decade of civil strife, Cromwell became commander of the parliamentary armies. He became Lord Protector in 1657, and he ruled until his death on September 3, 1658. The British monarchy was restored soon after, in 1660.

teetered back and forth. But in 1629, Charles I dissolved Parliament and did not call another one for 11 years. In 1640, he was forced to call Parliament to raise taxes to pay for war-related expenses.

Civil strife followed. The fighting led to the execution of Charles I in 1649. Victorious military leader Oliver Cromwell and his advisers passed an act that abolished the monarchy and declared England a republic—a country led by representatives of the people rather than a king. Cromwell, who became known as lord protector, called several parliaments, but he was unable to create lasting stability. In fact, his death in September 1658 created further turmoil in the country, and subsequent leaders and assemblies also failed to bring lasting peace. In 1660, the House of Lords and the House of Commons agreed to invite Charles I's heir, Charles II, to reclaim the throne.

Turmoil continued, and religious strife in England between Catholics and Protestants led to the 1688 invasion of England by Dutch ruler William of Orange, who forced the ruling leader King James II to flee to France. Parliament offered the monarchy to William and his wife, Mary, in 1689, which is also when Parliament first put forward its Declaration of Rights. The declaration outlined the liberties afforded to Parliament as well as the right to free speech. These rights became law when they were passed in December 1689 as an act of Parliament. They are now known as the Bill of Rights.

*William of Orange became the king of England in 1689.*

## Medieval European Parliaments

Although the British Parliament has a well-known history, the United Kingdom is not the only country to claim a representative body that stretches back into medieval times. Other regions of Europe, including Germany, Sicily, and parts of the Spanish peninsula, had developed representative assemblies in the thirteenth century. Iceland and the Isle of Man claim the oldest parliaments, which began as early as the tenth century.

Much like the United Kingdom's Parliament, most of these assemblies were called together by rulers, princes, kings, and even Catholic Church leaders who needed the advice, money, and military aid that society's elite could provide. Those who participated in these assemblies were of high social status. They were nobles, high-ranking clergy, and powerful local leaders and merchants. Even though these parliaments were not groups that truly represented the country's people, they became a way for rulers to learn about the people's needs and opinions.

These assemblies became entrenched throughout much of Western Europe in the four-teenth and fifteenth centuries. Countries such as Sicily, Iceland, Denmark, Ireland, and Poland all had some version of parliamentary gatherings during medieval times. However, power generally

## ICELAND'S PARLIAMENT PLAINS

Iceland is home to one of the world's oldest parliaments. Some historians consider it the oldest parliament in the world. The Vikings who had settled on the island just on the edge of the Arctic Circle came together in 930 AD to form a parliament called the Althing. The Althing met for two weeks every year at Thingvellir, a natural amphi-theater found in the island's southwest section. *Thingvellir* literally means "Parliament Plains." A speaker presided over sessions, which deliberated on a variety of issues, includ-ing Iceland's decision to adopt Christianity in 1000 AD. Viking chieftains often resorted to bat-tling each other at Thingvellir to enforce decisions or settle differences. The Althing general assembly continued to convene at Thingvellir until 1798. It is now a national shrine.

remained in the hands of the ruling monarchies. Only a few countries, such as Denmark, Sweden, and Switzerland, allowed representation drawn from the peasant class or allowed peasants to vote.

## Parliamentarianism Spreads

Although parliamentarianism is firmly rooted in European history, today parliaments are found in all areas of the globe. Many of the non-European nations that have parliamentary governments today are former British colonies, such as Australia, Canada, and India. Similarly, many African nations with parliamentary governments were once ruled by European countries that imposed their government systems on their colonies.

Not all non-European countries established parliaments as a result of colonial rule by European nations. Japan is one example. Various rulers, including nobles and military governors known as shoguns, controlled the island nation for centuries. Although they only hold nominal power now, Japan's emperors have been a constant force in government for 1,500 years. The country's government underwent a radical transformation in the nineteenth century. Ito Hirobumi, a clan leader who had studied in Europe, helped develop a parliamentary government as well as a constitution in the 1880s.

In addition to reaffirming the emperor's right to rule Japan, the constitution established a parliament known as the Imperial Diet. Japan's parliament had a House of Peers, made up of aristocrats, and a House of Representatives, whose members were chosen by a select group of taxpayers. Japan's first parliament had constitutional restrictions on its power. The country's creation of the Diet in the nineteenth century made Japan a leader among parliamentary governments in Asia, and other countries in that region created their own parliaments in the subsequent century.

The first parliaments generally lacked a sense of broad representation, and their powers were a fraction of what they are today. Yet these early assemblies laid the foundation for the modern parliamentary government. Their histories shaped how countries understand government, how citizens view their representatives, and how power is balanced among leaders and the people they strive to represent. Understanding such histories provides insight into the customs and policies that dominate the various parliaments in place today. ⌘

## AT A GLANCE: JAPAN

- An electoral democracy.
- The parliament is known as the Imperial Diet.
- The lower chamber is the 480-seat House of Representatives, comprised of elected representatives.
- The upper chamber is the House of Councilors, comprised of 242 elected members.
- The prime minister is the leader of the majority party or coalition in the House of Representatives. The prime minister serves as the head of government and appoints a cabinet of ministers.
- Emperor Akihito is the ceremonial head of state.

# 4

# All Parliaments
# Are Different

The parliamentary governments of the
world share many similarities. Generally,
parliaments have the power to name the prime
minister, who leads the government. In general,
parliaments also have some way of expressing
confidence or no confidence in their prime
ministers, thereby affirming or dissolving the
government.

However, parliaments can differ significantly
in how they are set up as well as how they
operate. Many parliaments consist of a single
house, or group of legislators, sometimes known

*For most of its history, the citizen-
elected House of Commons had
little influence in the affairs of
the British government.*

as a chamber. A government that has a single legislative body is called a unicameral system. Other nations have a bicameral system, which means their parliaments consist of two houses. Meanwhile, some nations have parliaments as well as monarchs. Others have a parliament and a president. Most countries with parliaments are democracies, but some are dictatorships or authoritarian states that do not have truly representative governments.

Cultural, historical, and political factors work together to determine how a parliament is set up, how it functions, and how it assigns the various duties of running the government. The British Parliament exemplifies how these factors played into the development of the bicameral system that is in effect in the United Kingdom today. The House of Lords, one of the two houses of the British Parliament, has existed for centuries. The members of the House of Lords are unelected, and most are appointed by the monarch. In previous centuries, the lords came from the British aristocracy. Now they come from the country's elite achievers as well as the aristocracy. The aristocracy provided support and advice for kings and queens for centuries. That is why the House of Lords held significant power and elected the prime minister for most of its history, from its medieval creation up into the twentieth century.

The House of Commons had members who were elected by citizens. But for centuries, average citizens wielded little if any power or influence. So for most of its history, the lower house had less power than the House of Lords. But as British citizens demanded more rights and asserted their desire for a more democratic system, the House of Commons became more and more powerful. The prime minister is now the leader of the party or coalition of parties that control the House of Commons. The House of Lords has been reduced to a secondary power with a strong advisory role. A new law can begin in either house. Both houses generally must approve legislation. But in some circumstances, the House of Commons can pass laws without the consent of the House of Lords, and the House of Lords cannot stop laws regarding taxes or government spending.

## The Bicameral System

As the name implies, a bicameral legislature has two chambers. One chamber is often called the lower house. The second chamber is called the upper house. For example, the House of Commons in the British Parliament is called the lower house, while the House of Lords is called the upper house. The US Congress also has two chambers, the House of Representatives and the Senate.

Generally, members of the lower chamber are elected. Upper chambers usually have fewer members than the lower chambers, and countries fill the seats in different ways, through elections, appointments, or inherited titles. Sometimes the members represent certain geographic regions, as is the case in Germany's upper chamber, the Bundesrat. When the upper house is geographically based, sometimes the members are appointed by the local governments of their regions rather than elected.

The lower and upper houses in each parliamentary system are not always equal in power. Many parliaments have stronger lower houses, including the British Parliament, the French Assembly, and the Japanese Imperial Diet. However, some systems have stronger upper houses that have the power to delay or void legislation passed by the lower houses.

Bicameral systems have a few distinct advantages. They often better represent diverse groups. They also encourage more debate over legislation, which may help create better laws overall. By having two chambers, they can often provide greater oversight of the prime minister and the cabinet. However, because bills and other legislative acts must pass through two chambers, bicameral systems can be slower to take action than unicameral systems. They can also be less accountable to their constituents, as

## A SAMPLING OF COUNTRIES WITH BICAMERAL PARLIAMENTS

- Australia
- Austria
- Belgium
- Canada
- Germany
- India
- Ireland
- Italy
- Japan
- Poland
- South Africa
- Spain
- Switzerland
- Thailand
- United Kingdom

members of one chamber can blame the other chamber for problems. Bicameral systems can also cost taxpayers more money, as citizens need to pay for more members and their staff.

## The Unicameral System

A unicameral system refers to a government that has a legislature with one chamber. This type of parliamentary system is often found in countries where government power is mostly in one central unit, rather than those that have many states or provinces. Countries that have a unicameral system include Israel and New Zealand. Countries with one-chamber legislatures tend to be geographically small too.

These one-chamber legislatures can often enact legislation quickly because only one chamber needs to debate and vote on the proposed laws. Legislators may also have greater accountability to their constituents in unicameral systems

**A SAMPLING OF COUNTRIES WITH UNICAMERAL PARLIAMENTS**

- Albania
- Bangladesh
- Denmark
- Finland
- Greece
- Hungary
- Israel
- Kuwait
- Lebanon
- New Zealand
- Norway
- Portugal
- Singapore
- Sweden
- Turkey
- Ukraine

because they cannot blame another chamber for inaction on proposals or bad outcomes on passed legislation. However, the disadvantage of a unicameral system is that it is more prone to passing flawed legislation than a bicameral system because legislation only has to make it through one legislative body rather than two.

## Monarchies and Parliament

Many parliamentary governments have separate offices for the head of government (the executive) and the head of state (a symbolic and ceremonial leader). In many parliamentary governments, the head of state is a monarch.

## AT A GLANCE: NEW ZEALAND

- An electoral democracy.
- The United Kingdom's Queen Elizabeth II is the head of state, but she is represented by a governor-general in New Zealand.
- The prime minister is the head of government and is the leader of the majority party or coalition of parties.
- The parliament has one chamber, the House of Representatives. Its 120 members are elected for three-year terms.
- Seven seats are reserved for the native Maori population.

- There are two main political parties in New Zealand. They are the Labour Party and the National Party.
- The government recognizes the rights and freedoms common to most Western democracies, including freedom of speech, press, and religion.

The government of the United Kingdom is one of the leading examples, but it is far from the only country that has a parliament and a king or queen. Japan has an emperor or empress and a parliament. European countries such as Belgium, Denmark, the Netherlands, Norway, Spain, and Sweden have both. Many Middle Eastern countries, including Bahrain, Jordan, Kuwait, Oman, Saudi Arabia, and the United Arab Emirates, also have a monarchy and a parliamentary government.

> "The Emperor shall be the symbol of the State and of the unity of the people, deriving his position from the will of the people with whom resides sovereign power."[1]
>
> —*Article 1 of the Japanese Constitution*

The role that each monarch plays relative to its parliamentary assembly varies. Today, most of the world's monarchs rule in a constitutional monarchy, which means they must operate within the boundaries established by a constitution. Generally, monarchs have limited power. They usually play a role as head of state. They often have the responsibility of asking the leader of the ruling political parties to form a government, and they have the responsibility of dissolving parliament. Some monarchs are more authoritarian and have the ability to bend their parliaments to their will.

# Dictatorships and Parliaments

Monarchs are not the only ones who can rule countries and their parliaments in an authoritarian manner. Throughout history, presidents, military leaders, and other national leaders have often seized or usurped power. When they choose to operate within an existing parliamentary system, this creates a parliamentary government that has no real power. Dictatorships often maintain parliaments even though the so-called parliaments have little or no sway over the dictator.

In some cases, keeping a parliament improves the world's opinion of the dictator. From the outside of the country, it can be

## AT A GLANCE: JORDAN

- The ruling monarch is King Abdullah II.
- The king appoints and dismisses the prime minister and cabinet. He can also dissolve the parliament, called the National Assembly.
- The country is not considered an electoral democracy, and many freedoms that Western democracies have, such as freedom of the press, are curtailed in Jordan.
- The National Assembly has two chambers. The 110-seat lower house is called the Chamber of Deputies. The 55-seat upper house is the Senate.
- Members of the Chamber of Deputies are elected, while members of the Senate are appointed by the king. Members in both chambers serve four-year terms.
- The Chamber of Deputies can approve, reject, or amend legislation proposed by the cabinet, but it has limited ability to initiate legislation. Islam is the state religion.

difficult to tell how the power relationship functions. Keeping a powerless parliament sometimes makes the rest of the world believe a country is more democratic than it really is.

In other cases, the parliament and the country's leader came to power with true democratic intentions, but later became corrupted. One-time democratic dictators have often rewritten their constitutions to allow them to stay in power. Parliaments can also rewrite the rules to their own benefit. For example, the Ugandan parliament has been accused of corruption and mismanagement. In 2009, it passed a law saying members would not have to pay taxes. Observers warn that the Ugandan government is too tightly linked to the military.

Parliamentary members often still have to secure their seats through elections. Some political parties maintain control of their parliaments through fraud or voter intimidation. In some nondemocratic governments, citizens vote only for candidates drawn from a ruling party or an elite or select class. Average citizens are often unable to break into the privileged class of individuals who can run for office. In other cases, citizens turn in ballots but all candidates run unopposed. Voters can vote yes or no for a candidate, but they cannot choose among multiple candidates.

Citizens exposed to such quasi-parliamentary bodies begin to realize that governments can respond to the people and act in the people's interests. Although there might not be real competition for these seats, these parliamentary members might still feel some sway from the voters or some responsibility to improve their countries. If a member of an opposition party manages to win a seat in the government by rising above fraud and voter intimidation, even that single member can be a voice for the people in the otherwise nondemocratic parliament.

## Exceptions to the Usual Rules

There is no single collection of rules that govern how parliaments around the world are structured. Instead, each country establishes how it wants to form its government based on its history and culture. For example, Israel experimented with a different system for choosing its prime minister for a short time. Unlike other parliamentary systems, where the majority party or coalition parties select the prime minister, from 1996 to 2001, the citizens of Israel directly elected the prime minister. Since 2001, the president has called on the party leader with the best chances of forming a government to be prime minister.

South Africa is another country that has altered the typical parliamentary setup. In the South African system, the parliament does not have a prime minister. Instead, it has a president who is both head of state and head of government. The president is not elected as he or she is in the United States. The president is selected by the South African parliament, known as the National Assembly. The National Assembly can also remove the president through a vote of no confidence.

*The South African parliament is led by a president chosen by its members.*

## France's Mixed System

The government of France is unusual. It is often called a semi-presidential system, but it is also sometimes called a mixed system. This government was established by the Constitution of 1958 and is officially known as the Fifth Republic. It sets up a bicameral parliament. The upper house is called the Senate, and the lower house is the National Assembly. The National Assembly is popularly elected, and the Senate is elected by an electoral college made up of national and local politicians.

Similar to other parliamentary systems, the president is the head of state, and the prime minister is the head of the government. The prime minister and the cabinet members are responsible to the legislature. However, the legislature has a limited ability to force the prime minister and cabinet members from office. Thus, France's parliament has less power than many others around the world.

The president is an elected position. But unlike the head of state position in other

## CHARLES DE GAULLE AND THE FIFTH REPUBLIC

Charles de Gaulle played a leading role in modern French history. He was a wartime leader as well as a statesman who shaped the structure of the country's current government, known as the Fifth Republic. Charles Andre Joseph Marie de Gaulle was born on November 22, 1890, in Lille, France. He entered Saint-Cyr, a military academy, in 1910, and he served in World War I (1914–1918). He was wounded three times, captured by the Germans, and awarded the Legion of Honor. Following the war, he continued his military career. His military work gave him an up-close look at how the French parliament of the era

operated. He was not impressed with how often governments were removed from office.

De Gaulle fled to London after the Germans invaded France during World War II. He led the French resistance to the German occupiers from the United Kingdom. He became a political leader in France following the Germans' defeat. But the government in the decade after World War II was weak, and it collapsed in May 1958. At that time, de Gaulle founded the Fifth Republic, which remains in place today.

parliamentary governments, the French president has an active role in government and has significant power. For instance, the president can fire cabinet members and call elections for a new legislature, but the legislature cannot call presidential elections. The president can also call for a popular vote, called a referendum, on proposed legislation.

The differences in parliaments stem from a variety of factors, including history, customs, and current needs. These differences do not fundamentally change the nature of parliamentary government. Instead, they create various interpretations of the same system. Even though there are many varieties of parliaments around the world, nearly all of them have a similar goal: to govern their countries and their constituents fairly. ⌘

## AT A GLANCE: FRANCE

- An electoral democracy.
- The National Assembly is the lower house. It consists of 577 members elected to five-year terms.
- The upper house is the Senate. It had 343 seats from 2008 to 2010, and planned to raise the number of seats to 348 in 2011.
- The president and the prime minister both have a great deal of power in the government.
- The French constitution guarantees freedom of religion, and the country protects the right to free assembly and the freedom of association.

# 5

# Rights and Responsibilities

Considering that parliamentary systems span the globe, there is no single model or example of what a citizen's life is like under this type of government. Some countries expect citizens to be active participants in their government. They also award their citizens a great range of freedoms, such as the right to speak their opinions about the government and its leaders without fear of prosecution. Other countries limit the rights, roles, and responsibilities that they grant to their citizens, even though the countries have some form of a

*British citizens met with Prime Minister Gordon Brown in 2010 before the parliamentary elections.*

RIGHTS AND RESPONSIBILITIES

parliamentary government that theoretically is
meant to represent its citizens.

The role of citizens in parliamentary government is not limited to voting. In fact, voting is
only one of many ways in which a citizen can play
a role in government. Citizens are expected to
be informed on issues and voice their opinions to
their leaders. They are also expected to pay taxes
to fund parliament's actions, and they have the
right and responsibility to run for public office.
As a report by the Inter-Parliamentary Union
(IPU), an international organization of parliaments established in 1889, explained:

> The role of citizens in a democracy is not
> exhausted by the act of electing a government;
> they need to be continually engaged with it if it
> is to remain in touch with the people and their
> needs. A democratic parliament for its part will
> seek to foster a vibrant civil society and to work
> closely with it in finding solutions to problems
> facing the country, and in improving the qual-
> ity and relevance of legislation.[1]

## Rights and Freedoms

Citizens in most of the countries with parliamentary government enjoy the same types
of freedoms and rights that US citizens enjoy,
including religious freedom, the right to assemble, and a free press. These rights help keep the
government accountable to the people. These
countries must also balance the rights they give
their citizens with other factors, such as public
safety and protecting minority groups.

Similar to other democracies governed by parliamentary systems, Canada has enshrined the freedoms and rights of its citizens. Canada's Charter of Rights and Freedoms, a document created in 1982, establishes that all citizens have, among other civil liberties:

> (a) freedom of conscience and religion; (b) freedom of thought, belief, opinion and expression, including freedom of the press and other media of communication; (c) freedom of peaceful assembly; and (d) freedom of association.[2]

The charter also establishes the right for citizens to vote, to remain or leave Canada freely, and to communicate with and receive services from parliament and the government.

## CITIZENS' RIGHTS WORLDWIDE

The United Nations' International Covenant on Civil and Political Rights establishes a long list of important liberties for citizens around the globe. The document in part says that:

> Every citizen shall have the right and the opportunity . . . without unreasonable restrictions:
>
> a. To take part in the conduct of public affairs, directly or through freely chosen representatives;
>
> b. To vote and to be elected at genuine periodic elections which shall be by universal and equal suffrage and shall be held by secret ballot, guaranteeing the free expression of the will of the electors;
>
> c. To have access, on general terms of equality, to public service in his country.[3]

In addition, Canada protects the rights of minority groups, including immigrants and native people.

In 2007, Canadian courts heard complaints from Muslims who claimed that published

## AT A GLANCE: CANADA

- An electoral democracy.
- Governed by a prime minister, a cabinet, and a bicameral parliament.
- The House of Commons has 308 members.
- Elections for the House of Commons must be held at least every five years.
- The Senate has 105 appointed members who can serve until the age of 75.
- The British monarch is the head of state but is represented by a ceremonial governor-general.
- The main political parties are the Conservative Party, the Liberal Party, the Bloc Québécois, and the New Democratic Party.

material in a magazine incited fear of Muslims. The case illustrated the difficulty in balancing the right of free speech and a free press with the need to protect minorities. The case was dropped, but the fact that it made it to court led some people to voice concerns that the government was interfering with a free press and the right to free expression of ideas.

At the same time, in the early twenty-first century, Canada also tried to balance its security concerns with its desire to safeguard its civil liberties. As a result, some laws passed by its parliament were later struck down or changed by its courts. In 2007, Canada's Supreme Court struck down a law that allowed police to arrest and indefinitely hold foreigners suspected of being terrorists.

## Handling Protest

Some parliamentary governments are stable, but others struggle and face political challenges and protests from their own citizens. Greece faced such a situation in 2010. Greeks protested in front of the parliament building as parliament members voted on proposals to deal with the country's financial crisis. The protests were

### CANADIAN LEADER: JEAN CHRÉTIEN

Jean Chrétien served as prime minister of Canada from 1993 to 2003, which made him one of the longest-serving leaders in the industrial world at the time. As Canada's twentieth prime minister and leader of the Liberal Party, Chrétien helped hold the country together and helped spur strong economic growth.

Chrétien was born in the province of Quebec on January 11, 1934. He entered politics when he was a teenager by campaigning for Liberal Party candidates. He went on to become a lawyer. In 1967, he started his service in the cabinet. He became prime minister in 1993 and governed three consecutive majority governments. He played an important role in a campaign against the 1980 and 1995 referendums that sought sovereignty for Quebec, the only French province in the otherwise English-speaking country.

He resigned as prime minister in 2003 and returned to practicing law. About his role in government, Chrétien said: "A prime minister has a unique duty to preserve the integrity of the office. It is not about power. It is about responsibility."[4]

sometimes violent. Police fired tear gas into the crowds and used stun grenades to try to disperse the protesters. The protesters responded by throwing bottles and stones at police. Despite the protests, members of parliament voted 172 to 121 in favor of a bill that would raise taxes and cut government spending.

The country's financial woes and the violent protests strained the government. A bombing on May 5, 2010, killed three bank workers. Prime Minister George Papandreou spoke against the violence and said the country's future was at stake. "The economy, democracy, and social cohesion are being put to the test," he said.[5]

Even though the bill passed in Greece's parliament, the political and social ramifications of the vote continued. Papandreou expelled three Socialist Party members from his team because they decided to abstain from voting. Thousands

## AT A GLANCE: GREECE

- An electoral democracy with a 300-member parliament.
- The parliament has only one house.
- The president, who serves a mostly ceremonial role, is elected by parliament to a five-year term.
- The president chooses the prime minister, who is usually the leader of the majority party in parliament.

- The Greek constitution provides for freedom of speech, freedom of the press, and freedom of religion, and it guarantees the right to assemble.

*Protesters against proposed spending cuts gathered in front of Greece's parliament building on May 5, 2010.*

of people continued their protests following the vote as store and business owners went to work boarding up burned buildings and cleaning up after the antigovernment riots.

Greece, which became a parliamentary republic in 1975, has seen social unrest and other threats to its stability in its recent history. Corruption scandals, charges of excessive police force, and prejudice against minority groups have prompted protests against the government and criticism from human rights groups. Yet the government protects the right of its citizens to assemble, and it maintains an independent judiciary. As part of a democracy with constitutionally protected rights, the Greek parliament—like nearly all democratically elected governments—has the duty to uphold its laws, including those that give citizens the right to protest.

## Citizenship in Nondemocratic Countries

Parliaments are also found in countries where freedoms, as Western democracies define them, are more broadly restricted. In those cases, the individual's rights, responsibilities, and roles in the government are often significantly different from those in more democratic countries, despite the common government system. According to the report entitled "Democracy in Southeast Asia," published in *CQ Global Researcher*, "True democracy is largely a fiction in Cambodia, Singapore, and Malaysia."[6] The government of Malaysia, for example, has restrictions on freedom of the media and the right to assemble. It would be nearly impossible for an opposition party to take control of the government—even though the country holds elections. Nondemocratic countries also frequently rig elections and other government processes so that much, if not most or all, of the public is excluded from participation. So while average citizens in democratic parliamentary systems can petition their representatives in parliament, protest, and even run for office, average individuals are generally excluded from such participation in nondemocratic parliamentary governments.

*Amnesty International has reported that the Malaysian police have the power to arrest peaceful protesters.*

Nondemocratic governments, whether they follow a parliamentary form or a different system, are also less open to the press and the public about issues. However, parliament can balance some of that tendency toward secretiveness. For example, when the global economy collapsed in late 2008 and recession took a worldwide hold through the subsequent few years, members of Malaysia's parliament criticized the ruling government (led by the royal family) for misusing public money and for failing to take adequate action to address the country's financial problems.

Democratic parliamentary governments, like other forms of democratic rule, give citizens a broad range of freedoms. They are free not only to live their lives without significant government interference or demands, but also to choose their level of participation in the system. Citizens have the right to vote, but they also have the right not to vote in many countries. Still, parliamentary democracies expect citizens to be active participants in the process. So while

## FREEDOM HOUSE REPORT

The parliamentary governments of several countries were criticized in a report from Freedom House, an international watchdog organization that promotes democracy around the world. The report, "Freedom in the World 2010: Erosion of Freedom Intensifies," found that Bahrain, Jordan, and Yemen had all suffered setbacks in the prior year.

The report downgraded the status of these countries, moving them from the category designated for countries where citizens were "partly free" to the category of countries where citizens were considered "not free." It reported that Jordan saw a loss of political rights "due to the king's decision to dissolve the parliament and postpone elections."[7] Political freedom in Bahrain "suffered as a result of the harassment of opposition political figures and discrimination by the minority Sunni elite against the Shiite majority."[8] Political rights in Yemen also declined because of "rapidly deteriorating security conditions and the increased marginalization of the parliament and other political institutions."[9] Morocco was not downgraded in status, but political rights also took a hit: "The increased concentration of power in the hands of forces aligned with King Mohammed VI, along with stepped-up harassment of opposition critics, increased concerns about the erosion of political rights in that country."[10]

they legally have the freedom to abstain from voting, parliamentary democracies expect citizens to understand the issues, voice their opinions on them, vote according to their beliefs, and even seek public office to advance those beliefs. These are the near universal ideals of parliamentarianism in regard to citizens' rights, roles, and responsibilities. ⌘

# 6

# A Stable Society

Parliaments govern. This sounds straightforward, but what does it mean to govern? What, exactly, are the functions citizens can expect of their parliaments? Like so many other facets of parliamentary government, the answers to these questions have changed over time. Even today, the answers vary from country to country. Some countries that have recently established parliaments may find their institutions are still fragile and their procedures for running parliament are still maturing. Other parliaments that have existed for centuries, such as the British Parliament, generally find they have well-established traditions as well as formal,

institutionalized rules for how they should operate.

Despite the numerous differences that exist among parliaments, parliaments worldwide do share many common functions. According to the IPU, parliaments have these basic functions:

- law making
- approving taxation and expenditure (generally in the context of the national budget)
- overseeing executive actions (the prime minister and cabinet), including policy and personnel appointments
- approving treaties
- debating issues of national and international concern
- hearing and redressing citizen grievances
- approving constitutional change[1]

These are all functions that can be seen in a typical parliamentary session. In the summer of 2010, for example, the British Parliament had several actions scheduled for review. It debated the economic impact of expanding a highway, published a report regarding the timetable for a voting reforms bill, held public sessions to learn more about a number of topics including education and monetary policy, and held a workshop on energy and the green economy.

# Creating a Stable Society

Parliamentary government often delivers stability too. For example, Germany had had some experience with parliamentarianism prior to World War II. But the country's historical parliaments were initially more regional, and the national tradition was weak. Still, the Germans opted to establish a parliamentary system for West Germany in 1949.

Prior to Adolf Hitler's Nazi regime, Germany had suffered from an unstable government under the Weimar Republic. The Weimar Republic was characterized by a fractured legislature in which no party was able to gather a majority. As coalitions splintered, the parliament was forced to hold frequent elections. This left the government unable to effectively govern, and soon Hitler's Nazi Party seized power. After the war, a new parliament system was designed to bolster some of the weaknesses of the older system. It brought stability to West Germany—officially known as the Federal Republic of Germany—for decades. West Germany became an industrial powerhouse. Government policy, especially budgeting, currency stabilization, and economic discipline, demonstrated by its central bank, was key in its economic success.

West Germany's parliament continued to be a stabilizing force as the country faced significant challenges through the twentieth century. The most notable challenge was the reunification of democratic West Germany with the former Communist state of East Germany in 1990. This event created difficult questions that parliamentary leaders needed to answer.

Those questions included how to create a parliament that could fairly represent an additional 15 million Germans and how to fairly represent the five additional states of the former, and poorer, East Germany in a reunified government. The West German parliament took charge. The Bundestag, its lower house, created a committee on reunification. Having this forum for debate and problem solving smoothed the reunification process. The countries were successfully reunited, and the German parliament adjusted to provide democratic representation for its combined citizenry.

## AT A GLANCE: GERMANY

- An electoral democracy.
- The country's constitution established a parliamentary system.
- The lower house of parliament is the Bundestag, with 622 members, who are elected at least every four years.
- The upper house, the Bundesrat, represents the states.
- The Bundestag and a group of state representatives choose the president, who is the country's head of state.
- The president's position is mostly ceremonial. The president can serve up to two five-year terms.
- The head of government is the chancellor. The Bundestag elects the chancellor, who usually serves for the duration of a four-year legislative session unless replaced by the Bundestag.

# Providing for the Masses

Making laws is one of the primary responsibilities of legislatures worldwide. However, legislatures, including parliament, are also tasked with providing services for residents of their countries. Many parliaments around the world end up providing a range of social programs as well. The British Parliament, for example, oversees an extensive list of programs that aim to care for its citizens. Using the money it collects through fees and taxes, it provides money to people who are unemployed. Since 1946, it has funded the National Health Service, which provides government-sponsored health care, including doctor visits and prescription drugs, for residents. It also provides money to senior citizens who have retired from the workforce.

Governments also provide money to pay for many of the services that people take for granted. They pay for the country's military protection. They pay for the creation and maintenance of roads. They subsidize public transportation, such as buses, subways, and trains. They help fund cultural institutions, such as historic sites and libraries. They help pay for education. The costs are significant, and parliaments in countries around the world spend many sessions debating how much money they should collect in taxes and fees as well as how much they should spend on these different programs. Each parliament comes to different conclusions about what to fund and how much it should pay.

# Setting Public Policy

Parliaments sometimes have to make difficult decisions that affect their citizens. How a parliament handles complex social issues varies. Each parliament is influenced by local factors, including whether the country is democratic or ruled by a small group, what values dominate its culture, the age of its population, and the tensions that exist among its citizenry. For example, when the French parliament discusses labor issues, it often comes under pressure from French trade unions. In 2010, the National Assembly readied itself to discuss overhauling the national pension system, a system that funds workers' retirement. Government officials stressed an overhaul was needed because of the costs and debt associated with the current system. At the same time, the country's leading unions called on workers and retirees to participate in strikes and demonstrations to protest any plans they thought might hurt workers. Parliamentary leaders often have to balance such competing factors when setting new policies.

Intense debate took place in France's National Assembly when it contemplated whether to ban the veils that some Islamic women wear over their faces. Many French citizens supported the ban on face-covering veils because they believe it goes against the French beliefs of secularism and equality for women. Face coverings can also pose a public safety threat if they make it difficult to identify people. But others said a ban would infringe on the religious freedom of Muslims. Muslims make up 5 million of the country's population of 64 million, which gives France the largest Muslim population of any European country.[2] Parliament debated these different points. But in July 2010, it passed the ban, which bars face-covering veils in public spaces.

Parliamentary action is not always the final word on an issue, however. Most parliamentary democracies have constitutions to which they must adhere. When laws are passed in many parliamentary systems, the judiciary can overturn laws that it judges unconstitutional, similar to what happens in the United States.

## UNIONS AND INTEREST GROUPS

Many parliaments are swayed by the power of labor and trade unions. These are groups of workers from the same industry, profession, or trade who join together to lobby lawmakers and other policy makers for laws and policies that benefit their particular group. Many unions are closely related to political parties such as the Labour Party in the United Kingdom and the Socialist Party in France. How much influence and power the unions have depends on different factors, ranging from how the public views the groups' demands to how vocal and active they are when presenting their concerns and requests to the public and members of parliament.

Another way citizens can band together to support causes and government actions is by joining interest groups, which have become much more powerful forces in modern political times. These groups represent a variety of issues, from environmental concerns to minority rights to issues particularly important to women. What is common across the spectrum, however, is their ability to reach members of parliament and sway the way in which they vote.

A parliament must be able to accomplish many difficult tasks for its citizenry. Representatives usually find themselves balancing the different and conflicting demands and opinions of constituents as they try to pass laws, pass budgets, and approve regulations. Yet most parliamentary governments manage to successfully navigate these demands and make decisions that represent what the majority of their citizens wants. Parliaments govern by majority rule, which helps to ensure that the will of the

## UNION LEADER: LECH WALESA

Unions and their leaders have had significant impacts on government dealings throughout history. One of the most notable union leaders of the twentieth century was Polish labor leader Lech Walesa. Born in 1943, Walesa became an electrician in a shipyard. He was fired in 1976 because of a leadership position he held within a labor union as a shop steward.

He led a strike in 1980 as workers demanded more rights. The strike forced government authorities to give workers the right to strike and organize their own unions. In 1981, he became chairman of the Solidarity union. However, the Communist government of Poland put a stop to Solidarity's activities and arrested Walesa later that same year. The 1980s were turbulent, but Walesa continued to gain international support. He also won a Nobel Peace Prize in 1983. He and other activists forced the Communist government to hold democratic parliamentary elections for the first time in 1989. In December 1990, he was elected president, and he served in that position until 1995. Today, Poland is a democratic country with a bicameral National Assembly, where the president appoints the prime minister.

*French citizens protested against raising the retirement age from 60 to 62 as part of the country's pension overhaul.*

majority prevails. When parliaments fail to do that, the people have the ability to replace them with members who they believe can serve them better and make wiser decisions. ⌘

# 7

# Fair Representation

The IPU states that, "the first criterion of a democratic parliament is that it should be representative of the people."[1] For that to happen, according to the IPU, the parliament must reflect what it calls the popular will. That means the parliament should be made up of the representatives chosen by the voters and the political parties must act and vote in a manner consistent with the beliefs they presented to their constituents. A democratic parliament should also reflect the people it serves "in terms of gender,

*Ballot boxes awaited counting in the 2003 election in the Philippines, which included migrant workers' votes due to a recent parliamentary change.*

language, religion, ethnicity, or other politically significant characteristics."[2]

## A CHECKLIST FOR TRUE REPRESENTATION

Freedom House is an independent watchdog organization that promotes freedom around the world. As part of its mission, it analyzes how well governments represent their people. As part of its *Freedom in the World 2010* Checklist Questions, it asked the following questions about the functioning of government:

*1. Do the freely elected head of government and national legislative representatives determine the policies of the government?*

*2. Is the government free from pervasive corruption?*

*3. Is the government accountable to the electorate between elections, and does it operate with openness and transparency?*[3]

Sometimes a parliament represents neither the popular will nor the social diversity of its country. A country's electoral system—the system through which candidates are chosen and votes are collected and counted—may be flawed, leading to the election of candidates and parties who do not represent the country's voters. The way the parliament selects representatives might be skewed to certain groups of voters. The constitution or the government might even deliberately shut out certain groups of voters.

Whatever the reason, a parliament that does not fairly represent the people of its country could become a destabilization force, rather than an entity that brings stability to its citizens. When groups do not feel part of the process, they are less likely to participate, creating further alienation and discord that can lead to civil strife. According to the "Parliament and Democracy in the Twenty-first Century: A Guide to Good Practice" report from the IPU:

*A parliament that is significantly unrepresentative in this respect, whether through deficiencies in electoral procedure or the electoral system, will to that extent forfeit legitimacy, and be less able to reflect public opinion on the important issues of the day.*[4]

In Thailand, violent protests erupted against the sitting parliament and its prime minister in 2010. The protesters were mostly poor, and they come from rural areas. They supported former prime minister Thaksin Shinawatra, who was ousted by a military coup in 2001 and was later convicted of corruption. They believed the elite dominated political power in their country and the powerful ignored the

"Parliament . . . is not a congress of ambassadors from different and hostile interests; . . . but Parliament is a deliberative assembly of our nation with one interest, that of the whole, where, not local purposes, not local prejudices, ought to guide, but the general good. . . . You choose a member, indeed, but when you have chosen him, he is not a member of Bristol, but he is a Member of Parliament."[5]

*—Edmund Burke, British statesman, 1729 to 1797, speaking on how the members of parliament must work together for the common good of the country*

poor, who made up the majority of voters. Even after a violent crackdown on the protesters in mid-2010, the political situation in the country remained unresolved and tense.

## THE INTERNATIONAL COVENANT ON CIVIL AND POLITICAL RIGHTS

The International Covenant on Civil and Political Rights was created by the United Nations. It guides countries on holding free and fair elections. The covenant says all citizens should have the right and the chance to:

a. participate in the conduct of government either on their own or through their freely and openly elected representatives;

b. vote in elections that are held regularly, open to all, and run by secret ballot to ensure the ability to vote without intimidation;

c. and have access in a fair and equal way to serving in the government of their country.[7]

## Methods for Inclusiveness

How a parliament becomes a fair representative of the popular will and the social diversity of its country is a complex matter. Different countries approach the issue using different methods and solutions. Generally, they consider the composition of the parliament and how representatives come to sit in parliament. According to the IPU, the "first and most basic is the guarantee of fair electoral procedures, to ensure that no voters, candidates or parties are systematically disadvantaged or discriminated against."[6]

At times, parliaments will look at their own composition, for example, in terms of ethnicity or gender, to determine if they are really representative of those whom they serve. If they do not believe they are representative of their people, some parliaments will make adjustments. For instance, some countries have adjusted their voting laws to allow citizens living abroad a vote. The Philippines amended its voting laws in 2003 to allow migrant workers living outside of the country to vote.

## Women in Government

Some governments have also established a set number of their members of parliament to represent specific groups, such as ethnic clans, minorities, or women. For example, some of the countries that have constitutionally mandated quotas for women include Bangladesh, India, and Uganda. Such countries often reserve seats in parliament for women, guaranteeing a minimum number of women will be in parliament. However, women can also win other seats as well, which might raise the number of women in those parliaments above the minimum. In other countries, including Denmark, Norway, and Sweden, political parties have developed a quota system to ensure that they put forward adequate numbers of women candidates.

A report from the Quota Project, a collaborative effort of International Institute for Democracy and Electoral Assistance, the IPU, and Stockholm University, found that quotas are an effective way to boost women's representation in parliaments worldwide. The report found that without the use of quotas, countries tend to see only a slow increase in the number of women serving in parliament. Because of this, the report found that many countries and organizations believe some mechanism is needed to bring more women into government: "Quotas present one such mechanism. . . . The hope for a dramatic increase in women's representation by using this system is strong."[8]

Women achieved a victory in the Middle Eastern country of Kuwait in April 2006 as they cast their vote for the first time. The 2006 election was for a single district seat that had been vacated while parliament was still in session. The election also marked the first time women could run for a seat in parliament. Two women were among the eight candidates vying for the vacant seat. Neither woman

## AT A GLANCE: KUWAIT

- The emir (monarch) is the head of state and shares legislative power with the National Assembly.
- The emir sets the political agenda, appoints the prime minster and cabinet, and can override the legislature. Although it has a parliamentary National Assembly, the small Persian Gulf country is not considered an electoral democracy.
- The National Assembly has 50 members who are elected to four-year terms by popular vote.
- The emir can dissolve the National Assembly at will. However, he must call elections within 60 days.
- Formal political parties are banned.

*Kuwaiti women voted for the first time in Kuwait's history in the 2006 elections.*

won. However, four women did win seats in 2009, making it the first time in the country's history that women won seats in parliament.

The National Assembly, the country's parliament, approved universal suffrage in 2005. However, the country required women and men to use separate polling booths, something demanded by the more conservative and traditional members of the Kuwaiti parliament.

"It's certainly a historical moment for me. I felt very happy while casting my vote. . . . I feel that justice has been achieved for Kuwaiti women," one woman told a reporter outside a polling station.[9] The advancement of women in politics in Kuwait mirrored changes happening in a number of Middle Eastern countries, which had banned women from politics as well as other aspects of public engagement throughout the twentieth century.

## Electoral Systems

A majority of the countries with a parliamentary system are democratic. They are considered electoral democracies because they hold national popular elections. But how the votes are counted and distributed can vary. There are multiple systems, and even when two countries use the same system, differences still remain.

In a plurality system, often called First Past the Post, the candidate who receives the most votes wins the district, even if the candidate did not capture the majority of the votes, or more than half. The United Kingdom uses this system, which is often used in countries in which a single member of parliament represents a specific district. This system tends to shape a country into a two-party system, which makes it difficult for third parties to win. In a majority system, a candidate must win a specific percentage of votes to win. Often it is a majority of the votes. If no candidate wins the set percentage in the first round of voting, two or more of the leading candidates face off for a second round, often called runoff voting. It is easier for independent candidates or third parties to win in this system.

In plurality or majority systems, a political party can win the highest percentage of votes in the election yet fail to take the highest number of seats in the parliament. This has happened in the United Kingdom a few times in recent history. In 1951 and 1974, the party that had a smaller percentage of votes overall actually had a larger number of seats in Parliament than the party that had the greater percentage of votes. And in 1992, the Conservative Party won only 42 percent of the votes yet took 52 percent of the seats in Parliament, making it the majority party with the ability to select the prime minister and form the ruling government.

Another common system used to elect parliaments is proportional representation (PR), which is used in countries such as Denmark, Finland, the Netherlands, Portugal, Spain, and Sweden. Although there are different types of PR systems, they are essentially designed to make the percentage of votes that a party receives match the percentage of seats in the legislature. PR systems often allow for multiple parties to win seats and lead to the formation of coalition governments.

Some countries, such as Germany and New Zealand, used mixed systems, where some members of parliament are selected using a plurality or majority system, while other members are chosen under the PR system.

# Failure to Represent

In some countries, a greater concern than the electoral system is whether parliament is representative at all. Just because a country has a parliament does not mean that country meets the standards of an electoral democracy. For example, Persian Gulf countries such as Bahrain, Kuwait, and Oman have both monarchies and parliaments. These countries held elections for national parliaments during the first years of the twenty-first century, but questions lingered about whether the elections and resulting parliaments fairly represented the people. In Kuwait, for

## PROPORTIONAL REPRESENTATION

A report from the ACE Electoral Knowledge Network highlighted the advantages of proportional representation and found that countries using the system:

• *Faithfully translate votes cast into seats won . . .*

• *Encourage or require the formation of political parties or groups of like-minded candidates to put forward lists. . . .*

• *Give rise to very few wasted votes. . . .*

• *Facilitate minority parties' access to representation. . . .*

• *Encourage parties to campaign beyond the districts in which they are strong or where the results are expected to be close. . . .*

• *Are less likely to lead to situations where a single party holds all the seats in a given province or district. . . .*

• *Lead to greater continuity and stability of policy. . . .*

• *Make power-sharing between parties and interest groups more visible. . . .*[10]

example, women were not allowed to vote or run for office until 2005. And in Bahrain, parliamentary "districts are drawn in a way that seriously under-represents the country's majority Shiite population," according to the Michael Herb's 2004 report, "Parliaments in the Gulf Monarchies: A Long Way from Democracy," in the *Arab Reform Bulletin*.[11] As the twenty-first century started, the Sultanate of Oman still had ultimate authority, even over the country's parliament. In addition, all three parliaments had only limited ability to block laws proposed by the monarch. ⌘

# 8

# Parliaments and Economies

J ust as there are no two parliaments exactly alike, there are no two countries with exactly the same economic systems. Countries that have parliamentary governments are just as diverse in their economic models as they are in their languages, cultures, and politics. Each parliament makes its own laws and sets its own policies about what it wants from its economy as well as what restrictions on business it believes best fit its needs.

As is true for all governments, parliamentary governments must set policies that promote

*A country's parliament can affect its currency's exchange rate.*

We Sell

| Country | Rate |
|---|---|
| AUSTRALIA | 0.8264 |
| BRAZIL | 0.5263 |
| CANADA | 0.9677 |
| CHINA | 0.1417 |
| Costa Rica | 0.0023 |
| Euro | 1.4093 |
| HONG KONG | 0.1412 |
| JAPAN | 0.0094 |
| MEXICO | 0.1014 |
| NEW ZEALAND | 0.7284 |
| S Korea | 0.0012 |
| SINGAPORE | 0.6922 |
| Sweden | 0.1502 |
| Switzerland | 0.8837 |
| TAHITI | 0.0123 |
| TAIWAN | 0.0342 |
| THAILAND | |

their economies. They must respond to problems. They decide how trade will be conducted with other countries. Because the economy is of the utmost importance to citizens, the success of a democratic parliamentary government rests in the success of its economic policies. If a party's economic policies become unsuccessful, it is in danger of losing power in parliament.

## How Governments Affect the Economy

Government decisions affect the economy in a variety of ways. For example, the government sets the interest rates charged on loans, tax rates, and policies. Government decisions also affect the economy through laws and policies that regulate industries of all types. In the United Kingdom, for example, former prime minister Margaret Thatcher came to power on a platform that sought to improve the country's economy by moving certain industries, such as the utilities and mining operations, from government control to private ownership.

How and where governments choose to spend money affects the overall economy. For example, in the spring of 2010, the parliamentary government of Greece warned that it might default on part of its debt. The news panicked investors around the world, who feared that the problems in Greece could end up affecting other countries as well as the international banks that lent Greece and other countries money.

One government's decisions can also affect other countries or the global economy. Countries can choose to trade relatively freely with others, encouraging global trade, or they can set policies that make trade with other countries more expensive, encouraging trade within their borders instead. In 2010, when the German parliament cut incentives for people and businesses to install solar panels to produce solar energy, the share prices of solar panel companies in other countries dropped significantly. Investors in these

## MARGARET THATCHER, THE IRON LADY

One of the most notable world leaders of the late twentieth century was British prime minister Margaret Thatcher. Thatcher entered the House of Commons in 1959 and became prime minister in 1979. She brought significant changes to the United Kingdom's economy by privatizing key industries. For example, the telephone and gas industries, the ports, and the airlines went from being owned by the government to being owned by private companies.

Her policies helped the United Kingdom enjoy economic growth. There were cuts in personal income taxes and a significant drop in inflation during the first six years of her tenure. However, support for her economic policies waned toward the end of her 11 years as prime minister. Thatcher's foreign policies, which aligned with US interests but stood firmly against European integration, also became increasingly unpopular. Opposition to her policies ultimately forced her resignation in 1990. Still, her legacy earned her the title of the Iron Lady. The impact of Thatcher's economic policies led to a new social category: "Thatcher's Children," referring to citizens who entered college or the workforce as she implemented her conservative economic platform.[1]

non-German companies feared that the companies would have less business in Germany, one of the world's biggest markets for solar panels, as a result of the cut incentives.

## Parliaments and Economic Problems

When the global economy collapsed in 2008 amid worldwide banking problems, the tiny Arctic island nation of Iceland and its parliament were suddenly big news. Iceland's economy tanked, and in the process, it ruined the nation's banks and sent the value of its currency plummeting.

## ECONOMIC SYSTEMS

Two basic types of economies are capitalism and socialism, which in theory are opposite to each other.

- Capitalism. This system allows individuals to decide how they want to handle their finances—including how to invest, what to buy or sell, what prices to charge, and how to operate their businesses. This system calls for a limited government and limited restrictions on that individual freedom.
- Socialism. In this system, the government controls the means of production,

such as natural resources, farms, and factories, and plans the economy.

However, in the real world, most governments have a mixed economy that takes elements from both systems. In a mixed-market economy, individuals are free to operate within restrictions set by the government. The government also plays an important role in setting regulations to protect the economy as well as individuals.

Icelandic citizens blamed their parliament in part for its lack of action, and they vented their frustration at their leaders through a series of protests. The parliament established a special commission to examine the collapse of the country's banking system. In 2010, the commission issued a report that said a number of Icelandic leaders, including the former prime minister, had been negligent.

Iceland's parliament was not the only one under fire when the world plunged into recession in 2008. Protesters in Bulgaria, Latvia, Lithuania, and Russia also took aim at their parliamentary leaders, blaming them for not doing enough to prevent the economic slide and for doing too little to help citizens hurt by the recession. The financial crisis became a political threat to more than one government. For example, the largest party in the ruling coalition in Latvia called for early parliamentary elections after large protests in January 2009.

## AT A GLANCE: ICELAND

- The island nation gained independence from Denmark in 1944.
- It established itself as an electoral democracy through its 1944 constitution, which gave power to the president, a prime minister, a unicameral parliament called Althing, and a judiciary.
- Members of the legislature are elected to four-year terms, as is the president.
- The president appoints the prime minister, who is responsible to the legislature.

*Protests broke out in Reykjavik, Iceland, over the government's handling of the economy.*

## Economic Promises

In a democratic parliamentary system, many political parties and their prime ministers come into power because of their economic policies and campaign pledges. If they cannot keep their promises, they may lose control of the government again through a vote of no confidence.

India held elections in 2004. The country had experienced significant economic growth in the 12 months leading up to the election, but the rising economy did not benefit the poor. The Congress Party promised to redirect spending. Such promises helped the Congress Party defeat the ruling Bharatiya Janata Party in the May 2004 elections.

It was not easy to keep that promise, however. New prime minister Manmohan Singh, who had previously served as finance minister, wanted to expand the economy quickly so there would be enough new jobs to employ the millions of unemployed Indians. But the prime minister also had to do so without spending a lot of money.

Past Indian governments had made strategic decisions that put the country on an upward economic trajectory. Government leaders put resources into promoting higher education as a way to industrialize the country's business base. As a result, the country produced a large number of professionals, including those trained in computers and information systems. Similarly, government policies toward technology—for example, no taxes on software exports—helped spur the growth of information technology (IT) services based in India. Many of these IT services were sold to companies in other countries, including the United States. It was a business

## AT A GLANCE: INDIA

- An electoral democracy that achieved independence from the United Kingdom in 1947.
- The lower house of India's parliament is the 545-seat Lok Sabha, or House of the People. Most members are elected for five-year terms. The chamber also includes two appointed members representing Indians of European descent. The Lok Sabha determines the leadership and composition of the government.

- Most members of the 250-seat upper house Rajya Sabha, or Council of States, are elected by state legislatures. They serve staggered six-year terms. Up to 12 members can be appointed. State and national lawmakers choose the president, who plays a mostly symbolic role as head of state. The president serves a five-year term.

arrangement known as outsourcing or offshoring, and it created thousands of well-paying jobs for educated Indians.

However, India's governments had to contend with lingering problems that kept the country from even more extensive economic growth. The government borrowed money to pay its bills, and as a result, it accumulated large deficits. It also spent a significant amount of money subsidizing agriculture and energy.

## GLOBALIZATION AND SOVEREIGNTY

A significant trend that emerged in the late twentieth century and continued into the next century was globalization. At its most basic level, globalization means the development of markets and networks that allow for a free exchange of ideas and goods across national borders. Globalization is often used in an economic or business sense, but organizations such as the European Union and the United Nations show how globalization also brings nations together politically. In an era of globalization, national governments have been tasked with balancing their own country's interests, the concerns of their own citizenry, and the demands of the global marketplace.

A number of factors will determine how globalization turns out in the future. Some of those factors are the labor supply, the cost of resources such as electricity, and the overall business climate. However, governments have a significant role to play in shaping the future of globalization. For instance, parliaments might enact laws that hinder globalization by favoring business transactions within their own borders. Parliaments could also form treaties with other governments that create more open economic markets, which could increase globalization by lifting restrictions that hinder business dealings across those borders.

The Congress Party and its allies who formed the ruling coalition government that took over in 2006 laid out a plan to address some of those problems. The new government worked to reduce lingering political and military tensions with neighboring Pakistan as a way to attract more investors to India. It undertook regulatory and tax reforms, which encouraged the country's business community. It also started to reduce the budget deficit, even as it expanded spending in rural areas. The United Progressive Alliance, the coalition led by the Congress Party, also won the 2009 parliamentary elections, allowing Singh to remain as prime minister.

Whether a government is a parliamentary system or another form, it can dramatically affect its own domestic economy, the economies of other countries, and the global economy as a whole through the decisions it makes. While all governments have the ability to impact the economy, democratic parliaments, like all democracies, generally do not consider only monetary issues when making economic policies. Parliaments must balance economic considerations against the other factors that matter to the government and the people they represent. So a decision on whether to pay for certain incentives, such as solar energy in Germany, is considered not only in terms of cost but also in terms of its affect on the country's overall fiscal health, its taxes, and the values of its people. In this way, parliaments make economic policies that are representative of the people they serve. ⌘

# 9

# International Relations

**A**ll governments—parliamentary and other—must interact with the other nations of the world. They must consider trade, immigration and citizenship, alliances, and disputes with other nations. Although they will go to war to protect their national interests, most countries with democratic parliamentary systems use diplomatic measures to solve conflicts. Many are part of international organizations that promote peace or trade among their members. Nondemocratic parliamentary systems are often less stable and less peaceful. The international community

*At its headquarters in Budapest, the Hungarian parliament debated an issue affecting international relations with Slovakia.*

occasionally intervenes with economic sanctions or even military action when provoked by nondemocratic countries.

## Citizens of Hungary

In June 2010, the Hungarian parliament voted on a proposal about citizenship. It decided to grant Hungarian citizenship to ethnic Hungarians who live in the countries that border Hungary. The vote would allow approximately 3 million ethnic Hungarians living in Romania, Serbia, Slovakia, and Ukraine to become Hungarian citizens if they could prove they were of Hungarian origin and could speak Hungarian.

Three months prior to the vote, the Fidesz Party had won in Hungary's April elections with a two-thirds majority. Granting citizenship to ethnic Hungarians in the bordering nations had been a campaign promise.

### AT A GLANCE: HUNGARY

- Once part of the Austro-Hungarian Empire, it became an independent country after World War I. It was occupied by Soviet troops after World War II and fell under authoritarian Communist rule.
- Reforms in the 1980s led to free parliamentary elections in 1990, and now the country is an electoral democracy.
- There is a 386-seat unicameral National Assembly.
- The National Assembly elects the prime minister and the president, whose duties are mostly ceremonial.

The response from other nations to the Hungarian parliament's vote was not positive, however. The Slovakian parliament called the law a security threat. Slovak prime minister Robert Fico said Hungary was "egotistic and arrogant" to pass the law without consulting his country, considering 500,000 ethnic Hungarians live in Slovakia.[1] In response to the Hungarian law, the Slovak parliament passed legislation that would take Slovak citizenship away from anyone who is granted citizenship in another country.

Hungarian foreign minister Janos Martonyi insisted that the Hungarian legislation did not affect Slovakia. He said the Slovak government was creating a political storm in advance of its own parliamentary elections. Still, some members of the Hungarian parliament said the dispute with Slovakia could cause problems for the ethnic Hungarians who lived in that country.

## Beyond Its Borders

As Hungary's citizenship law shows, the actions that any one parliament takes can have repercussions outside its nation's boundaries. The repercussions can be tied to issues of national security, as in the case of Slovakia's objections, or they can be economic.

When Greece faced its economic crisis in 2010, its parliament's response openly considered how other countries would view its potential default on its loans as well as what other nations could do to help. Leaders were clear about the country's need to rely on other nations. "The only way to avoid bankruptcy and a halt on payments is to get this money from our European partners and the IMF," Finance Minister George Papaconstantinou told parliament.[2]

## International Pressures and National Sovereignty

Parliaments around the world have to balance their national interests and their desire to preserve their sovereignty with the needs and opinions of other nations. The Israeli parliament has been in that position multiple times since its formation in 1949. It found itself in that situation again in 2010. The Israeli government imposed

## AT A GLANCE: ISRAEL

- Formed in 1948 when Israel declared independence.
- It is an electoral democracy.
- There is a unicameral parliament called the Knesset, which has 120 seats.
- The Knesset elects a president, whose duties are mostly ceremonial. The president serves a seven-year term.
- The prime minister is usually the leader of the majority party or the party that forms a coalition government.
- Israel bans certain political parties and candidates, specifically those that deny the existence of Israel as a Jewish state, oppose democracy, or incite racism.
- Freedoms typical of democratic governments, such as freedom of the press and freedom to assemble, are respected.

*In Finland, protesters marched on June 1, 2010, to show their opposition to Israel's attack of an aid flotilla.*

an economic blockade of Gaza, a Palestinian-controlled territory on the Mediterranean Sea, in 2007. As part of that blockade, Israel banned certain imports, such as construction materials, from entering the disputed region, where Palestinians and Israeli forces had battled for decades. The blockade drew intense international criticism in 2010 when Israeli commandos raided a flotilla carrying humanitarian aid that tried to break through the blockade. The raid left one US and eight Turkish citizens dead.

Initially, Israeli leaders gave no indication that they would bow to international pressure to end the blockade. In fact, Israeli prime minister Benjamin Netanyahu said the blockade was vital for Israeli security. But the Israeli cabinet was forced to respond following the event, and it entered discussions to abandon its three-year-old blockade. International observers speculated that the diplomatic pressure that other nations put on the Israeli government prompted the lawmakers to reconsider the issue. The pressure was significant. Allies such as the United States, other nations in the region including Turkey, and the European Union all weighed in on the matter, urging a resolution. The European Union is an international organization that consists of many of the countries of Europe. As 2010 closed, Israel

## ISRAELI STATESMAN: DAVID BEN-GURION

The first prime minister of Israel was David Ben-Gurion. Ben-Gurion was born in 1886 in what is now Poland. In 1906, he immigrated to Palestine, which was ruled by the Ottoman Empire. There, he helped establish agricultural communes until the Ottoman authorities deported him following World War I.

From Palestine, Ben-Gurion went to New York. He returned to Palestine as part of the Jewish Legion, a unit of the British Army, and he called for Palestine to become a homeland for Jews. He became active in political life and remained a vocal leader in the push for a Jewish land. In 1942, he joined others in calling for the creation of a Jewish state. After World War II, he declared his support for an armed struggle to support Jewish immigration to the region. On May 14, 1948, Ben-Gurion declared the foundation of the modern state of Israel. He led the Jewish people in Israel's successful war of independence following the declaration, which had prompted surrounding Arab armies to invade. He served as prime minister and minister of defense from 1948 to 1953 and then again from 1955 to 1963.

remained adamant in maintaining key aspects of its blockade.

The events in 2010 were not the first time that Israel had to answer to international scrutiny of its blockade. The European Union had been critical of the blockade for quite a while. The blockade had also been a perennial issue in Egypt. After the flotilla incident, Egyptian president Hosni Mubarak saw pressure grow from Egyptian citizens who wanted to end the blockade.

## Common Interests

Because they share similar histories and governmental values, many parliamentary governments have joined together in a variety of international organizations. For example, the countries that once made up the British Empire are part of an organization known as the Commonwealth. This organization's roots go back to 1867, when Canada became the first of the British Empire's colonies to become a self-governing dominion. In 1884, a British politician saw changes in the British colonial holdings and described the empire as a "Commonwealth of Nations."[3] Australia, New Zealand, South Africa, and the Irish Free State all became dominions in the first 22 years of the twentieth century. The prime ministers of these countries met in 1926 and defined *dominions* as autonomous countries, with none being subject to another. But they acknowledged that they were "united by common allegiance to the Crown, and freely associated as members of the British Commonwealth of Nations."[4]

Today, there are 54 sovereign nations in the Commonwealth. There are 19 in Africa, 12 in the Caribbean, ten in the South Pacific, eight in Asia, three in Europe and two in the Americas. The countries are home to 2 billion citizens. This association has some powers. Each country's government has agreed that the Commonwealth Ministerial Action Group (CMAG), a group of nine foreign ministers, has the power to determine whether a country goes against the Commonwealth nations' core values of "democracy, freedom, peace, the rule of law and opportunity for all."[5]

The CMAG can punish countries that go against these values. The Commonwealth also works through diplomatic channels to resolve any conflicts or problems. In addition, prime ministers from the Commonwealth nations meet regularly, as do many of the cabinet members.

## Cooperative Agreements

Another organization that brings together parliamentary governments is the Inter-Parliamentary Union, or IPU, which is based in Geneva, Switzerland. Established in 1889, its goal is to establish "world-wide parliamentary dialogue and works for peace and co-operation among peoples and for the firm establishment of representative democracy."[6]

According to the IPU, the organization provides a forum where parliaments and parliamentarians of the 155 member countries can exchange information and ideas, discuss issues, promote human rights, and contribute "to better knowledge of the working of representative institutions and to the strengthening and development of their means of action."[7]

## International Censure

Nondemocratic parliamentary governments are often scrutinized by the international community. The outside world watches for human rights abuses, rigged elections, or the early stages of military action. The IPU works to promote increased democracy among its members, which include such countries as China, Cuba, and North Korea where democracy does not flourish.

## CHINA'S PARLIAMENT

China is governed by the Chinese Communist Party, which came to power in 1949. It is a single-party, authoritarian country that does not tolerate political dissent. It does not recognize the freedoms most democracies guarantee, such as free speech. In those regards, China is different from many other countries with parliamentary governments. It has a 3,000-member National People's Congress, or NPC. Members are elected to serve five-year terms by regional congresses. The NPC elects a president who can serve up to two five-year terms. The NPC also confirms the premier, also called the Chinese prime minister, after he is chosen by the president. But the NPC does not hold real power, as it meets only two weeks a year to approve proposed legislation.

One measure used by the international community to encourage change in nondemocratic countries is economic sanctions. These sanctions usually involve forbidding all trade or certain types of trade with the country being penalized. The United Nations (UN) imposes sanctions on countries, as do individual nations.

In June 2009, the UN reaffirmed ongoing sanctions against Iran. The UN was concerned that Iran was trying to build nuclear weapons and contended that Iran was not cooperating

## AT A GLANCE: IRAN

- The government has a mix of elected and appointed officials. Iran is a theocracy, and Islam is the supreme law of the land.
- The parliament and the president, the head of government, are elected by the people. However, the candidates are approved by the Guardian Council, an unelected body appointed by the Supreme Leader and the judiciary.
- The head of state, the Supreme Leader, is appointed by the Assembly of Experts. This assembly is elected, and its members must be clergy and must be approved by the Guardian Council.

- The parliament, the Majlis, has 290 members elected every four years. The Majlis passes laws, subject to the approval of the Guardian Council.
- The president is the second-most powerful leader, after the Supreme Leader. The president is responsible for ensuring the constitution is followed. The president is elected separately from the parliament.

with UN nuclear inspectors. Iran argued that it wanted to build nuclear reactors in order to use nuclear power in its country and that it was not pursuing nuclear weapons. The sanctions forbid other countries from selling weapons to Iran and put restrictions on financial transactions related to a potential nuclear program. ⌘

# 10

# Benefits of a Parliamentary System

There are important benefits and strengths inherent in a parliamentary system of government. For instance, a parliamentary system can help guarantee representation for diverse groups, either by requiring quotas in parliament membership or by allowing multiparty systems to flourish. The parliamentary system can also help ensure internal stability within a country because it represents its citizens. Scholars debate, however, whether a parliamentary system is

*Parliamentary elections, such as the 2007 election in Ukraine, are considered particularly responsive to voters.*

better in delivering these benefits than other democratic forms of government, such as the presidential system used in the United States.

"As the central institution of democracy, [parliaments] embody the will of the people in government. . . . As the elected body that represents society in all its diversity, parliaments have a unique responsibility for reconciling the conflicting interests and expectations of different groups and communities through the democratic means of dialogue and compromise. . . . Parliaments have the task of adapting society's laws to its rapidly changing needs and circumstances. . . . [and] they are responsible for ensuring that governments are fully accountable to the people."[1]

—*"Parliament and Democracy in the Twenty-First Century: A Guide to Good Practice," from the IPU*

## Responsive to Voters

One benefit parliamentary government may have over other forms is how well it reflects the will of the country's voters. The government in power must have at least a majority of the seats in parliament. So from the start, the legislative branch generally reflects what a majority of the voters want. Since the prime minister and the cabinet nearly always come from members of the majority party or coalition parties, the executive branch also reflects what a majority of the voters want.

Parties must hold a majority of seats in a parliament in order to form a government, or else they must join with other parties to form a coalition government. As a result, parties that represent diverse, yet small, portions of the population are sometimes asked to join in running the government. Thus, that segment of the population has a more visible and powerful voice than it likely would have in other types of governments.

Similarly, some parliaments can guarantee representation of their diverse populations by stipulating that a set number of parliamentary seats are reserved for particular groups. Some

## QUOTAS IN RWANDA

Rwanda saw brutal ethnic violence in the 1990s, when Hutu extremists tried to eliminate Tutsis and moderate Hutus, leaving as many as 1 million people dead. The country entered a new era in 2003 with a new constitution and national elections. In 2010, Rwanda could boast that its parliament had the highest percentage of women of any parliament in the world. Women held 56.3 percent of the seats in Rwanda's parliament, passing Sweden's 47.3 percent. Rwanda's figures far surpassed the worldwide average, too, which showed that women constituted only 18.4 percent of the members of parliaments around the world in 2010. Rwanda's success in getting women into parliament was a result of its use of quotas to guarantee gender balance.

However, Rwanda is not considered an electoral democracy. International observers deemed that the presidential and parliamentary elections in the first decade of the twenty-first century gave Rwandan citizens only a limited degree of political choice, and restrictions on freedom of the press and speech blocked full access to political life.

*Angela Merkel became the first female chancellor of Germany in 2005.*

countries—Rwanda, for instance—require a minimum number of women members. Other countries designate seats for ethnic minorities.

## Cooperation, Flexibility, Stability

Some scholars also point to the fused executive and legislative branches as a benefit. Because the prime minister and cabinet come from the ruling majority party or the parties that form a governing coalition, the executive branch and the legislative branch generally agree on economic policies, foreign relations, and domestic initiatives. There is little or no inaction or grid-lock due to disagreement between the legislative and executive branches, which is a problem that sometimes plagues presidential systems. In fact, in some parliamentary systems, such as in the United Kingdom, where the prime minister is a particularly powerful political figure, party discipline is strong. When a single party holds the majority of the seats, the prime minister can expect nearly all of his or her legislation to pass.

Another perceived benefit to the parliamentary system is its flexibility. Members are elected to serve a term of usually four or five years. Members often serve terms that are shorter because elections can be called before their terms are up. In most cases, this is the accepted system, and it provides no real disruption to the continuity of the government. The parliamentary system allows for representatives and prime ministers to call for new elections to replace current members at nearly any time, not just when their fixed terms are over. So if members of the minority party in parliament believe the government no longer represents the will of the people, they can call for a vote of no confidence in the prime minister and force a new election. Or if members of the majority party or coalition parties believe the prime minister is no longer effective, they can remove and replace that leader without an election.

Such a move happened in Japan in the summer of 2010. The lower house of the Japanese parliament, the Imperial Diet, replaced Hatoyama Yukio as prime minister with Kan Naoto after

Kan took leadership of the governing Democratic Party. The move came after Hatoyama was criticized for poor political leadership and when his approval ratings plunged below 20 percent for failing to deliver on an election promise.

A parliamentary system can also bring stability to the country it serves. The fact that the government's prime minister can be replaced when he or she becomes ineffective or moves away from the party's platform of policies allows for a quick, yet usually peaceful, transfer of leadership. With a peaceful way to change government, revolutions or coups are less necessary. This ability to change leadership without an election can also help keep prime ministers from seizing more power than is constitutionally or customarily allowed. The result in both cases is that a need to change leadership does not have to lead to a crisis that could topple the government completely.

## Benefits in Nondemocratic Countries

A parliamentary system can be beneficial in countries that are not truly democratic. When elections are controlled by the people in power, citizens might not have much choice of candidates. They must often select candidates from an elite or select class or candidates from a single party. If elections are rigged, votes are not counted fairly. Still, citizens at least have some say in who gets into office, which can sometimes influence the direction of the country.

In nondemocratic countries that have no parliament, average citizens are often completely shut out of the process, leaving only a limited number of privileged individuals to select the country's leaders.

It is clear that parliaments in dozens and dozens of countries around the world fulfill their missions to represent and serve the citizenry of their nations. Each country comes to that mission through different procedures, including different election systems or quotas to ensure fair representation. In most cases, parliamentary government demonstrates its strengths through how well it has worked and continues to work for numerous nations. ⌘

## REPRESENTATION IN CHINA

The Communist Party exercises authoritarian rule in China, holding the elected National People's Congress (NPC) in a subordinate role. However, citizens derive benefits from their NPC representatives, even though the NPC lacks the power to take action independent from the Communist Party and meets for only two weeks each year. As a Chinese report to the IPU explained, there are benefits to having a short legislative session: "This has enabled them to have direct interaction with the voters, feeling their pains and understanding their aspirations. . . . They also assist in the implementation of the Constitution and the laws in their production, work, and social life."[2]

# 11

# Criticisms of a Parliamentary System

**P**oliticians in Turkey undertook an interesting debate in the spring of 2010: Would a presidential system bring more democracy to the Middle Eastern country, or could it lead to a dictatorship?

The debate came as the Turkish parliament considered a number of constitutional amendments. In the midst of that debate, Turkish prime minister Recep Tayyip Erdoğan said the country should consider switching to a presidential

*Japan's prime minister, Kan Naoto, took office in June 2010. The ability to replace the prime minister is a strength and a weakness of the parliamentary system.*

system. Erdoğan said a presidential system would eliminate the conflict in authority that exists between the prime minister and the president. Burhan Kuzu, a law professor and a deputy in Erdoğan's Justice and Development Party, raised another point: "In the parliamentary system, the legislative branch has no power because the executive branch dominates."[1]

The debate in Turkey raised questions about Erdoğan's motives for such a move. It highlighted the potential worry that a leader could make a presidential post authoritarian. But the discussion also demonstrated that politicians as well as political scholars see potential drawbacks in parliamentary systems. One drawback is the

## AT A GLANCE: TURKEY

- Turkey became a modern, secular republic at the end of World War I following the breakup of the Ottoman Empire.
- The country is considered an electoral democracy.
- As stipulated in its 1982 constitution, there is a 550-seat unicameral parliament called the Grand National Assembly. Members serve four-year terms.
- The directly elected president appoints the prime minister. Although the prime minister is head of government, the president has the power to veto legislation.
- The constitution protects the freedom of association and the freedom to assemble.
- The constitution also ensures freedom of religion. However, the role of Islam in public life has been a contentious issue in Turkish politics.

potential for instability, due to parliament's ability to force new elections at any time by showing no confidence in its leadership. Another potential problem lies in how the legislative and executive powers are merged, which means there are no checks and balances between the two branches of power as there are in a US-style presidential system.

## The Potential for Instability

Although the flexibility of the parliamentary system can bring stability by providing a process for the peaceful transfer of power, some scholars say it can also lead to instability. Members of parliament can call for votes of no confidence if they disagree with their prime minister's actions or believe he or she is ineffective.

## HITLER'S PARLIAMENT

Adolf Hitler, supported by his Nazi Party, ruled Germany and allowed for no dissent or opposition. His rule is an example of how a leader can quickly take dictatorial control. After taking power, the Nazis quickly outlawed all other political parties. The Nazis took away the parliament's power, but they did not disband the governing body itself. Parliament still held a handful of meetings, but all its members were Nazi Party officials. There was no debate in the Nazi parliament, and all laws were approved unanimously. Parliament remained a venue for Hitler to announce policy decisions and a public way to show the world Nazi control.

*Some blame Germany's weak government
after World War I for Hitler's rise to power.*

Some scholars have suggested that the
frequent elections in Germany during the Weimar
Republic in the 1930s were due in part to the
social unrest following Germany's defeat in World

War I and contributed to the rise of the Nazi Party. There were four elections between 1930 and 1933, which meant voters had little time for reflection, and the parliament had little time to accomplish its work. The lack of time for reflection, combined with voter frustration, helped Adolf Hitler and the Nazis gain more and more votes until they stamped out the democratic process.

In a less dramatic example, the Italian parliament does not generally see a single party

## AT A GLANCE: ITALY

- Italy replaced its monarchy with a republican form of government in 1946, and today it is an electoral democracy.
- The president, who has a mostly ceremonial role, is elected by parliament and representatives of the 20 administrative regions created by the constitution. The president serves a seven-year term.
- The president picks the prime minister. The prime minister is often the leader of the largest party in the lower house of the Italian parliament.
- The lower house is the Chamber of Deputies, which has 630 seats.
- The upper house is the Senate. It has 315 seats.
- A move in 2005 to use proportional representation in elections now means that the winning political party or coalition parties will have at least 54 percent of the seats in the Chamber of Deputies. The move was designed to create stability in a country that has seen more than 60 governments from 1945 to 2010.

take a majority of its seats. A coalition of parties is needed to form a ruling government and pick a prime minister. These coalition governments have proved to be very short lived. In fact, Italy has had more than 60 governments in office in the 65 years from 1945 to 2010.[2]

## Weakened Executive

The parliamentary system has also been criticized by some experts for its potential to create a weak executive office. A prime minister's authority is tied to parliamentary support. So a prime minister's power and effectiveness can be weakened by factors beyond his or her control. For example, a prime minister who presides over a coalition government made up of numerous or extremely diverse political parties might find it difficult, or even impossible, to reach consensus among the ruling parties. Following the formation of a coalition government in the United Kingdom in 2010, Patrick Manning, prime minister of Trinidad and Tobago, said that coalitions lead to "weak governments, [because] too many compromises have to be made on matters of policy."[3]

Critics of parliamentary systems also worry that prime ministers might fail to take unpopular but necessary actions for fear of forcing a no-confidence vote that could remove them from office. In contrast, in a typical presidential system, impeachment is such a difficult process that presidents can generally expect to finish their terms, so they have more freedom to take unpopular actions.

Additionally, some critics have faulted the parliamentary system for the way in which its heads of government are chosen. Prime ministers are not democratically elected by citizens, but rather chosen by the people who hold office. Some critics contend that prime ministers may see themselves responsible to only those members of parliament in the political party or coalition parties that put them in office. The prime minister may also be more strongly influenced by party leadership than a leader selected separately from the legislature, such as the US president.

## Lack of Checks and Balances

Although the parliamentary system has been criticized by some as having the potential for a weak executive, parliamentary government has also been criticized for its potential to have an executive branch—that is, a prime minister—that can operate without the same level of checks and balances found in other governmental systems, particularly a presidential model. For instance, if a prime minister wants to pass a particular piece of legislation, his or her political party is expected to back the measure. Officials within the political party often work behind the scenes to ensure that party members in parliament show strong support for the measures under consideration.

Similarly, some critics have found parliamentary systems flawed because there is no executive check on legislative power. Because parliament and the prime minister are codependent and the legislative and executive branches are fused, the prime minister presses for the measures and policies supported by the majority of parliament, just as a majority of parliament generally supports the prime minister. Contrast that with the balance of power in presidential systems, where the president is elected separately from the legislative branch and can support or oppose policies and proposed laws without fear of the legislators calling for a no-confidence vote.

## PARTY DISCIPLINE

Individuals called party whips help ensure that party members tow the party line. The party whips help make sure that party members actually vote in the chamber and vote the way the party wants. Whips also help party members get the opportunity to speak on proposals and important topics. Whips can also discipline members who do not support the party's agenda by denying them opportunities to speak or to hold committee positions.

## Party Politics

Parliaments operate using party politics. The political party or parties with the majority of seats form the government. According to some criticisms, this might create an environment in which party members in parliament do not assert themselves or their views on the issues. Party members, particularly those who belong to the ruling party, might not voice any disagreement with party leadership, the cabinet, or the prime minister, because they might be subjected to political isolation. Disagreement could threaten their own effectiveness as legislators as well as their ability to win reelection. Party members might also be reluctant to go against the party's stated positions and policies because they might fear the loss of promotion within the party ranks. Moreover, those who speak against the party's policy could face actual discipline from party officials and lose the opportunity to advance within the party.

Additionally, because of the need for strong party politics in a parliamentary system, representatives who are not part of existing political parties have little, if any, opportunity to become elected to parliament. Even if an independent candidate were elected, that individual would likely have little to no influence because the majority party or parties would not need his or her independent vote to pass legislation.

## REFORM AND RENEWAL

The need for reform is not exclusive to new or non-democratic parliaments. Well-established parliaments are subject to problems if they cannot or will not change with the times. The IPU notes:

> With regard to the long-established democracies, most see the main demo-cratic challenge and impetus for parliamentary reform as being the need to keep the institution relevant in the context of rapid social change and potential public apathy. "A major challenge", notes the Australian House of Representatives, "is keeping the parliamentary institution relevant to the needs and perceptions of the public it represents."[4]

*The party system is a strength and a weakness of parliamentary governments.*

The party discipline seen in many parliamentary governments is not much different from the party discipline that can often be found in US politics. However, discipline is usually stronger in parliamentary governments. Party cohesion is expected because the executive and the legislature are controlled by the same party. In addition, political parties in most of these countries control their nomination processes. In the United States, a primary election system selects candidates. US party leaders have little control over who gets the nomination.

Although the parliamentary form of government can trace its roots back approximately 1,000 years, the system still has its critics. These critics fault the structure of the system, in which the executive (the prime minister) and the legislature (parliament itself) are interdependent, so the relationship lacks checks and balances. They also point to the potential for instability and inadequate action as other possible flaws. Still, parliamentarianism remains one of the primary government forms and has carried numerous national governments through hundreds of years. The system may have potential problems, but it still remains a robust form of democracy. ⌘

# 12

# Parliaments in the Twenty-First Century

**V**oters in Afghanistan went to the polls on September 18, 2005, to vote in the first elections for their new parliament. Some 6.8 million citizens—or 57 percent of the 12.5 million people registered—turned out to vote in the election, which was supported by $160 million in international aid.[1] The election followed decades of warfare, civil strife, and repressive tribal leadership in the central Asian country.

---

*Many Afghan candidates advertised their campaigns for parliament in 2010, but the country's democratic government remained shaky.*

The new bicameral parliament consisted of a lower house, called the House of the People (or Wolesi Jirga), and an upper house, called the House of Elders (or Meshrano Jirga). The lower house had 249 seats, with 28 percent (or 68 seats) reserved for women. Voters elected their representatives for these seats. Meanwhile, seats in the upper house were filled by appointment. The president chose representatives for 34 seats, half of which were required to be filled by women. The councils that represent and help govern regional provinces, called provincial councils, chose representatives for 34 seats. The constitution called for the district councils—councils representing and running smaller regional areas called districts—to pick representatives for the remaining 34 seats. However, because the district elections had yet to be held, the provincial councils selected the district councils' 34 representatives to serve on an interim basis.

## Parliaments in Afghan History

Parliamentary government was not entirely new to Afghanistan. Following its independence from the United Kingdom in 1919, King Amānollāh organized an assembly. The country then adopted its first constitution, called Nezamnama. Following the constitution's enactment, the country in 1923 formed its first constitutional assembly, called the Council of State. This gave Afghan citizens a role in policy making for the first time. In 1931, the country adopted a new constitution, which called for elections to a new bicameral

National Assembly that had an elected chamber as well as a chamber of appointed members.

Through this time, the monarchy remained a strong institution. However, the adoption of another constitution in 1964 signaled a change in the balance of power. With the move to a constitutional monarchy, the king's powers were curbed and the powers of the bicameral National Assembly were strengthened. The Constitution of 1973 ended the monarchy altogether and created a republic system of government with a president as head of state.

## AFGHAN GOVERNMENT

Afghanistan is another example of the variety of ways democratic governments can organize themselves. The Afghan government features a bicameral parliament, but its head of state and head of government are combined in its president, who is directly elected by the people. This makes the Afghan system more similar to the US presidential system, despite the fact that its legislature is a called a parliament.

However, the first president was assassinated, the National Assembly disbanded, and the country was invaded by the Soviet Union. Even after the Afghans defeated the Soviets and pushed them out of their country, Afghanistan continued without any form of central government. Instead, the region was ruled by warring tribal leaders. In fact, there was no form of national democracy in Afghanistan until after the Bonn Agreement of 2001, which called for the formation of a new constitution and democratically elected officials.

How the new parliament will fare remained unclear as 2010 closed. President Hamid Karzai, who is both head of state and head of government, was taking on a particularly visible role in rebuilding the country and leading the new government. International observers charged that there were incidents of fraud in the 2009 presidential elections. Parliamentary elections scheduled for early 2010 were postponed until later in the year. This delay was caused by concerns about public safety and security as well as a lack of funds to pay for the election.

## A New Era for Parliaments

The creation of the new Afghan parliament was just one of the many changes taking place around the world at the start of the twenty-first century. Parliaments established in the last decade of the twentieth century in Eastern European countries, including Bulgaria, Hungary, and Poland, survived their initial years. They continued to uphold democratic principles as they entered the twenty-first century. The success of Kuwaiti women, who for the first time voted and ran for parliament, is an example of progress. Another example is Rwanda's parliament, which emerged from the aftermath of genocide. The fair and free election held in Bangladesh in 2008 also showed the promise of parliamentary government.

Iraq also instituted a democratically elected parliament in the early years of the twenty-first century after the US military and its allies forced dictator Saddam Hussein from power in 2003. Iraqis first voted for representatives to serve in the new 275-seat National Assembly in 2005. This National Assembly had significant tasks to accomplish. It had to pick a president, who would then appoint a prime minister. It had to draft a new constitution and find a way to govern a country that suffered decades of dictatorship, economic embargoes, wars, and internal ethnic strife. Still, there was hope among elected and government

## AT A GLANCE: BANGLADESH

- After free and fair parliamentary elections in 2008, the country became an electoral democracy. The country's official religion is Islam.
- A unicameral national parliament is composed of 345 members. Of those members, 300 are directly elected to five-year terms.
- The other 45 seats are filled by women nominated by political parties and then voted on by lawmakers. The number of nominations allowed per political party is based on each party's share of elected seats in parliament.
- The president is elected by parliament and serves a five-year term. The president performs mostly ceremonial duties.
- In 2008, the country lifted restrictions on the right to assemble and the right of free association.

leaders that the new Iraqi parliament could succeed. "This is going to be one of the most inclusive and certainly the most representative government in the history of Iraq," Foreign Minister Hoshyar Zebari told reporters following the election in February 2005.[2]

But similar to the situation in Afghanistan, the new Iraqi parliament faced an uncertain future. Another parliamentary election in 2010 led to months of debate about which parties would be able to form a coalition government and which political leader would fill the prime minister's position. As 2010 came to a close, the

## AT A GLANCE: RWANDA

- The country is not considered an electoral democracy.
- The president, who can serve up to two seven-year terms, has broad powers under the 2003 constitution. The president appoints the prime minister and has the authority to dissolve the Rwandan parliament.
- The parliament is bicameral. There are 26 seats in the upper house, or Senate. Each member serves an eight-year term. Twelve members are elected by regional councils, the president appoints eight members, a forum of political parties choose four

members, and universities have two representatives.

- The lower house is called the Chamber of Deputies. Fifty-three members are directly elected. Local councils chose 24 women. Youth and disability groups together choose three members.
- Although the constitution permits political parties to exist, it strictly controls them due to the constitution's emphasis on national unity.

debate continued to threaten the future security of the new parliament as well as the country itself.

## Crises and Challenges

The situation in the Middle East shows that although parliamentary government has been a successful and stabilizing force for hundreds of years in some countries, it cannot solve all the problems of a troubled country by itself. The stability of parliamentary governments in other regions of the world also came under threat in the first decade of the twenty-first century.

In early 2009, protesters in Iceland, upset about the government's handling of the country's economic problems, gathered outside the Althing parliament building on the government's first meeting of the new year. The protesters broke windows and set off smoke bombs outside. The protest forced politicians to barricade themselves inside the building for hours, but the demonstration was eventually broken up by the police, who fired pepper spray into the crowd.

Street violence and political strife rocked the Thai parliament throughout 2010, as an antigovernment group known as the Red Shirts forced lawmakers into debate over the group's demands, tactics, and future.

The Red Shirt movement, formally known as the United Front for Democracy Against Dictatorship, contended that Prime Minister Abhisit Vejjajiva came to power illegitimately. The protesters, mostly poor people who were loyal to an exiled billionaire, took over the streets of Bangkok, the country's capital. At another point, they stormed parliament, forcing the evacuation of government leaders. The protesters demanded that the prime minister step down and hold new elections.

The military cracked down on the protesters in May 2010. Approximately 100 people were killed, and more than 1,800 were wounded during the two months of protests and the military

## AT A GLANCE: THAILAND

- Thailand moved toward democratic rule in the 1980s, and elections held in 1992 started a 14-year period of elected civilian leadership.
- Civil and government discord threatened the government's stability, and an August 2007 vote that approved a new constitution implemented some nondemocratic provisions, such as reducing the role of elected lawmakers. An elected parliament remained intact, but the elections in 2007 were not considered free or fair.
- Under the 2007 constitution, the Senate has 76 elected members (who cannot belong to political parties) and 74 appointed by a committee of judges and members of independent government bodies.
- The House of Representatives has 480 seats. Members are elected to four-year terms.
- The prime minister is elected from the members of the House of Representatives. King Bhumibol Adulyadej is the head of state.

crackdown. Even after the crackdown, the Red Shirt movement continued to threaten the government as parliament became embroiled in the conflict. Debate among members of parliament became angry, and reconciliation between the opposing sides started to look impossible. Members of the opposition parties accused the ruling government party of unjustified violence against the protesters, while the ruling party accused the demonstrators of provoking violence.

As a result of the unrest, the government shut down Web sites and radio stations, a move that drew protests from some within parliament as well as human rights advocates elsewhere.

## The Future for Monarchies

War-torn countries were not the only places where parliaments experienced upheavals in the early twenty-first century. Some countries with parliamentary systems and monarchs as heads of state also had uncertain futures.

In 2007, the future for the king of Nepal was insecure. Members of Nepal's interim parliament held an emergency session to debate the future of King Gyanendra. One of the former parties that made up the coalition government, the Maoists, demanded the immediate abolition of the monarchy and wanted it replaced with a Communist state. The governing Nepali Congress Party, which also favored a republic instead of a monarch, wanted the issue taken up instead by the next parliament. The king was actually dethroned in 2008.

Nepal was not alone in its debate over the future of a monarchy. Average citizens and parliaments in other countries also wondered whether their countries should abolish their monarchies. For example, a poll taken in 2010 in Sweden found that a growing number of citizens wanted to see the monarch abolished, mostly because supporting the monarchy costs taxpayers money. Even though opposition to the monarchy had more than doubled in a decade, 58 percent of Swedes favored keeping the monarchy.

## The European Parliament

The start of the twenty-first century also saw a new powerhouse parliament increasing in visibility and importance: the European Parliament. The European Parliament is the directly elected body of the European Union. As of 2010, voters throughout the 27 member states of the European Union—a collection of countries that encompass 500 million citizens—elected the parliament's 736 members to serve five-year terms. The European Parliament and the Council of Ministers, which represents member states, set policy for the European Union. These policy decisions touch on many aspects of individual and national interests, including environmental protections, consumer rights, and transportation issues.

As it moves ahead, the European Parliament faces challenges in increasing democratic representation in its member nations. As these and other issues play out, the emergence of the European Parliament, the creation of new

*Members of the European Parliament vote on issues facing the organization's member nations.*

parliaments in developing countries, and the strengthening of others are indications that the twenty-first century will be significantly shaped by the policies, programs, and prime ministers that these governing institutions produce. ⌘

# Quick Facts

### Definition of Parliamentary Government

A parliamentary government is one in which the parliament has the power to make and execute laws. There are several different types of parliamentary governments, but the most recognizable form is the Westminster parliamentary model, which is used in the United Kingdom as well as other countries.

### Well-Known Countries with a Parliamentary Form of Government

Some parliamentary governments include: Australia, Canada, Denmark, Greece, Italy, Norway, Japan, South Africa, Sweden, and the United Kingdom.

### Organization of a Parliament

In a parliamentary government, legislative and executive powers are fused together. The prime minister is generally drawn from the ranks of the members of parliament. The prime minister is often the leader of the political party or coalition of parties that has the majority of seats in parliament.

### Main Leadership Positions

The prime minister is head of government. He or she sets the agenda for domestic and foreign policies and leads parliament in setting laws. The prime minister working with parliament is also responsible for the country's economic policies, including tax policies, budgeting, and spending figures.

The head of state, which is often a ceremonial post, is usually held by either a monarch or a president. Duties of the head of state depend on the constitution, customs, and laws of each country. For example, the president of France has much more political power than the queen of the United Kingdom.

## Founders and Advocates

No one individual developed the parliamentary system. Rather, the system evolved from democratic practices established first in ancient Greece and then developed in medieval Europe as kings called on noble leaders and later the emerging merchant class to provide advice, military aid and money. The United Kingdom is one of the best-known contributors to the rise of parliamentary government, but other European countries were important contributors to modern parliament government.

## Historic Leaders

- David Ben-Gurion, Israel (1948–1953, 1955–1963)
- Jean Chrétien, Canada (1993–2003)
- Oliver Cromwell, England (1653–1658)
- Charles de Gaulle, France (1959–1969)
- Ito Hirobumi, Japan (1885–1888, 1892–1896, 1898, 1900–1901)
- King John, England (1199–1216)
- Margaret Thatcher, the United Kingdom (1979–1990)
- Lech Walesa, Poland (1990–1995)

## How Power Shifts

Most parliamentary governments, but not all, have a democratically elected parliament. Elections are not held on a set schedule. Most countries require at least one election every several years; however, elections can be more frequent. The ruling party can call for an election if it thinks the situation is advantageous to enlarging its majority in the parliament. Or the ruling party could be forced to call one if the members of parliament have a vote that indicates they no longer have confidence in their leader. Some nondemocratic countries have elections to parliament but the average citizen may have little or no choice in representatives running for parliamentary seats.

## Economic Systems

Most of the countries with parliamentary systems have a market system based on capitalist principles. Examples include the countries of Europe as well as Australia, Canada, Japan, and South Africa. Many of these countries also have strong social programs where taxes pay for a strong network of social services such as health care and unemployment.

## The Roles of Citizens

Parliamentary governments are generally stable, and citizens' main responsibility is voting in parliamentary elections. In a democratic state, citizens vote for members of political parties or nonpartisan representatives. Although they do not directly elect the prime minister, citizens indirectly choose their government leader when they vote for members because the leader of the political party with the most seats generally becomes prime minister.

## Personal Freedoms and Rights

In most countries with parliamentary government, citizens have the types of freedoms long associated with Western democracies, including freedom of religion, freedom of association and assembly, freedom of speech, and the right to a free press. However, a parliamentary government does not always mean the government is democratic or free, and some countries with parliamentary government are more authoritarian with restrictions on many aspects of personal life. Citizens in some of these countries also find that although they have a parliament, their choices for representation are so limited that they essentially have no choice with their vote.

## Strengths of a Parliament

- Responsive to voters
- Legislature and executive work together
- Flexibility to call elections when leaders no longer are effective
- Stable

## Weaknesses of a Parliament

- Potential for weakened executive, particularly if there is a coalition government
- Few checks on executive power
- Few checks on legislative power

# Glossary

**abstain**
To refrain from participating, to refrain from doing.

**accountability**
To be held liable or responsible for one's actions.

**aristocracy**
A privileged class, often of inherited power, title, or wealth.

**authoritarian**
Nondemocratic rule by a state authority.

**civilian**
Of average citizens, not of the military.

**coalition**
A partnership, a union of different entities.

**constituent**
A voter; a citizen or resident served by a politician or institution.

**coup**
A sudden and absolute change of government either illegally or by force.

**enshrine**
To hold or establish as sacred or important.

**entrench**
To strengthen, fortify, or secure.

**fiscal**
Relating to finances, including spending, income, and debt.

**ideology**
Doctrines or opinions.

**judiciary**
Of judges and courts.

## lobby
To persuade or influence someone to agree with a particular point of view.

## recession
A decline in prosperity.

## repercussion
The consequences of an action or event.

## sovereign
The state of being independent from all other rule.

## statute
A law passed by a legislative body.

## subsidize
To aid or support with money.

## usurp
To seize without authority, to take control without legal right.

# Additional Resources

## Selected Bibliography

Haggard, Stephan, and Mathew D. McCubbins, eds. *Presidents, Parliaments, and Policy.* New York: Cambridge UP, 2001. Print.

Helms, Ludger. *Presidents, Prime Ministers and Chancellors: Executive Leadership in Western Democracies.* New York: Palgrave MacMillan, 2005. Print.

Laver, Michael, and Kenneth A. Shepsle, eds. *Cabinet Ministers and Parliamentary Government.* Cambridge, UK: Cambridge UP, 1994. Print.

Lipset, Seymour Martin, and Jason M. Lakin. *The Democratic Century.* Norman, OK: U of Oklahoma P, 2004. Print.

## Further Readings

Cain, Timothy M. *The Book of Rule: How the World is Governed.* New York: DK, 2004. Print.

Field, John. *Story of Parliament: In the Palace of Westminster.* London: Third Millennium, 2002. Print.

Magstadt, Thomas M. *Nations and Government: Comparative Politics in Regional Perspective.* Belmont, CA: Wadsworth/Thomson, 2005. Print.

## Web Links

To learn more about parliaments, visit ABDO Publishing Company online at **www.abdopublishing.com**. Web sites about parliaments are featured on our Book Links page. These links are routinely monitored and updated to provide the most current information available.

## Places to Visit

**UK Parliament**
Westminster, London, United Kingdom
www.parliament.uk
The UK Parliament offers a limited number of tours for overseas visitors during the summer. The Web site features a virtual tour of the buildings that house the British government.

**United Nations Headquarters Building**
First Avenue and Forty-Sixth Street
New York, NY 10017
212-963-8687
www.un.org
The United Nations Headquarters Building is open to the public and offers tours.

# Source Notes

### Chapter 1. A Parliament Renews Itself

1. "Full Text: David Cameron's Speech to the Conservative Conference 2005." *guardian.co.uk*. Guardian News and Media Limited, 4 Oct. 2005. Web. 24 Oct. 2010.

2. "David Cameron and Nick Clegg Pledge 'United' Coalition." *BBC*. BBC, 12 May 2010. Web. 24 Oct. 2010.

3. Ibid.

4. "Cameron Says Deficit Is Even Worse Than Thought as He Warns Debt Charges Could Top £70bn." *Mail Online*. Associated Newspapers, 7 June 2010. Web. 24 Oct. 2010.

5. Ibid.

### Chapter 2. What Is a Parliamentary Government?

None.

### Chapter 3. Parliaments in History

1. Eric Voegelin. *The Collected Words of Eric Voegelin*. Ellis Sandoz, Gilbert Weiss, and William Petropulos, Eds. Columbia, MO: U of Missouri P, 1998. *Google Book Search*. Web. 24 Oct. 2010.

2. "Featured Documents: The Magna Carta." *National Archives & Records Administration*. US National Archives & Records Administration, n.d. Web. 24 Oct. 2010.

### Chapter 4. All Parliaments Are Different

1. "The Constitution of Japan." *Prime Minister of Japan and His Cabinet*. 3 May 1947. Prime Minister of Japan and His Cabinet, n.d. Web. 24 Oct. 2010.

## Chapter 5. Rights and Responsibilities

1. "Parliament and Democracy in the Twenty-First Century: A Guide to Good Practice." Chapter 1. *Inter-Parliamentary Union.* Inter-Parliamentary Union, n.d. Web. 24 Oct. 2010.

2. "Canadian Charter of Rights and Freedoms." *Department of Justice.* 29 Mar. 1982. Department of Justice Canada, 18 Oct. 2010. Web. 24 Oct. 2010.

3. "International Covenant on Civil and Political Rights." *Office of the United Nations High Commissioner for Human Rights.* 16 Dec. 1966. OHCHR, 2007. Web. 25 Oct. 2010.

4. "Jean Chrétien." *CBC News.* CBC, 13 July 2009. Web. 28 Oct. 2010.

5. "Greek Parliament Votes in Favour of Austerity Measures." *BBC.* BBC, 6 May 2010. Web. 24 Oct. 2010.

6. Barbara Mantel. "Democracy in Southeast Asia." *CQ Global Researcher* 4 (1 June 2010): 131–156. Web. 14 July 2010.

7. Arch Puddington. "Freedom in the World 2010: Erosion of Freedom Intensifies." *Freedom House.* Freedom House, July 2010. Web. 25 Oct. 2010.

8. Ibid.

9. Ibid.

10. Ibid.

## Chapter 6. A Stable Society

1. "Parliament and Democracy in the Twenty-First Century: A Guide to Good Practice." Chapter 1. *Inter-Parliamentary Union.* Inter-Parliamentary Union, n.d. Web. 25 Oct. 2010.

2. "French Parliament Approves Law to Ban Burkas, Despite Criticism from Muslims and Human Rights Groups." *Daily News.* NY Daily News, 13 July 2010. Web. 25 Oct. 2010.

## Chapter 7. Fair Representation

1. "Parliament and Democracy in the Twenty-First Century: A Guide to Good Practice." Chapter 2. *Inter-Parliamentary Union.* Inter-Parliamentary Union, n.d. Web. 24 Oct. 2010.

2. Ibid.

3. "Freedom in the World 2010 Checklist Questions" *Freedom House.* Freedom House, 2010. Web. 25 Oct. 2010.

4. "Parliament and Democracy in the Twenty-First Century: A Guide to Good Practice." Chapter 2. *Inter-Parliamentary Union.* Inter-Parliamentary Union, n.d. Web. 24 Oct. 2010.

5. Legislative Council and Legislative Assembly. "Parliamentary Debates, Session 1904." Melbourne, Australia, 1905. *Google Book Search.* Web. 25 Oct. 2010.

6. "Parliament and Democracy in the Twenty-First Century: A Guide to Good Practice." Chapter 2. *Inter-Parliamentary Union.* Inter-Parliamentary Union, n.d. Web. 24 Oct. 2010.

7. Ibid.

8. "About Quotas." *quotaproject.* International IDEA, Stockholm University and Inter-Parliamentary Union, 2009. Web. 25 Oct. 2010.

9. Michael Herb. "Parliaments in the Gulf Monarchies: A Long Way from Democracy." *Arab Reform Bulletin.* Carnegie Endowment for International Peace, 20 Nov. 2004. Web. 25 Oct. 2010.

10. "Advantages of PR systems." *ACE: The Electoral Knowledge Network.* ACE Project, 2005. Web. 25 Oct. 2010.

11. "Kuwaiti Women Vote for the First Time." *BBC News.* BBC, 4 April 2006. Web. Oct. 25 2010.

## Chapter 8. Parliaments and Economies

1. David Hole, Le Zhong, and Jeff Schwartz. "Talking About *Whose* Generation?" *Deloitte Review* 6 (2010): 87. Web. 25 Oct. 2010.

## Chapter 9. International Relations

1. Stefan Bos. "New Law Granting Citizenship to Ethnic Hungarians Sparks Row with Slovakia." *DW-World.de.* DW, 25 May 2010. Web. July 2010.

2. Maria Petrakis and Natalie Weeks. "Greek Parliament Debates Budget Cuts as Nation Mourns." *Bloomberg Businessweek.* Bloomberg, 6 May 2010. Web. July 2010.

3. "History." *Commonwealth Secretariat.* Commonwealth Secretariat, n.d. Web. 25 Oct. 2010.

4. Ibid.

5. ibid.

6. "What Is the IPU?" *Inter-Parliamentary Union.* Inter-Parliamentary Union, n.d. Web. 25 Oct. 2010.

7. Ibid.

## Chapter 10. Benefits of a Parliamentary System

1. "Parliament and Democracy in the Twenty-First Century: A Guide to Good Practice." Chapter 1. *Inter-Parliamentary Union.* Inter-Parliamentary Union, n.d. Web. 24 Oct. 2010.

2. "Parliament and Democracy in the Twenty-First Century: A Guide to Good Practice." Chapter 4. *Inter-Parliamentary Union.* Inter-Parliamentary Union, n.d. Web. 24 Oct. 2010.

## Chapter 11. Criticisms of a Parliamentary System

1. Döndü Sariisik. "Turkey Debates Merits of Presidential System after PM's Comments." *Daily News & Economic Review.* Hurriyet Daily News and Economic Review, 20 Apr. 2010. Web. 25 Oct. 2010.

2. Selah Hennessy. "British Coalition Governments' Effectiveness Debated." *VOANews.com.* VOANews.com, 18 May 2010. Web. 25 Oct. 2010.

3. Richard Lord. "Manning: Coalitions Lead to Weak Govts." *Guardian Trinidad and Tobago.* Trinidad Publishing Company, 10 May 2010. Web. 25 Oct. 2010.

4. "Parliament and Democracy in the Twenty-First Century: A Guide to Good Practice." Chapter 8. *Inter-Parliamentary Union.* Inter-Parliamentary Union, n.d. Web. 24 Oct. 2010.

## Chapter 12. Parliaments in the Twenty-First Century

1. Kenneth Katzman. "Afghanistan: Politics, Elections, and Government Performance." *Congressional Research Service.* Congressional Research Service, 14 Sept. 2010. Web. 25 Oct. 2010.

2. "Shiite Alliance Wins Plurality in Iraq." *CNN.com.* Cable News Network, 14 Feb. 2005. Web. 25 Oct. 2010.

# Index